THROUGH
THE BANKS
OF THE
RED CEDAR

THROUGH THE BANKS OF THE RED CEDAR

My Father and the Team That Changed the Game

MAYA WASHINGTON

Published by Little A, New York

www.apub.com

Amazon, the Amazon logo, and Little A are trademarks of Amazon.com, Inc., or its affiliates.

ISBN-13: 9781542016674 (hardcover)
ISBN-10: 1542016673 (hardcover)
ISBN-13: 9781542016667 (paperback)
ISBN-10: 1542016665 (paperback)

Cover design by Adil Dara
Cover photo by Ed Bock

Printed in the United States of America

First edition

For

The Washington family of La Porte, Texas
The Goudeau family of McNair, Texas
The Smith family of Beaumont, Texas
And all pioneers who changed the game

When from these scenes we wander

And twilight shadows fade,

Our memory still will linger

Where light and shadows played

———

From "MSU Shadows,"

the Michigan State University alma mater

CHAPTER
ONE

We have a passing to note tonight. A star of sports and later the movies: Bubba Smith, born Charles Aaron Smith in Beaumont, Texas. The six-foot-seven-inch defensive standout for the Raiders, Oilers, and Colts. He went on to act in the *Police Academy* movies. Bubba Smith was 66.

—Diane Sawyer, *ABC World News Tonight*

My dad hopped a flight as soon as the funeral arrangements were made. *It would have been nice if he'd flown into LAX instead of Ontario airport,* I thought as the two of us started off onto the 57 freeway, just before rush hour, to pay our final respects to his childhood friend, Charles Aaron "Bubba" Smith, in Los Angeles. Fortunately, my mom's first cousin Benny was retired and lived in nearby Pomona. He met my dad at the airport, and they enjoyed some time together at Benny's home until I could get off work in Los Angeles.

Then in his early 70s, Benny had been a second father to me most of my adult life. Watching Benny age seemingly overnight had strangely prepared me for the life chapter my *actual* father was slowly creeping toward. The chapter where you attend more retirements than graduations. And more funerals than birthday parties.

Considering the circumstances that brought him to town in the first place, I did my best to remind myself that being stuck in traffic with my dad, who I hadn't seen in months and who was still alive at 66, wasn't the worst thing in the world. Even if he was determined to point out the obvious in that way that dads do.

"Ahh, shucks. Traffic. How do people drive like this every day? Look at all these cars," he declared from my passenger seat.

I wanted to remind him that he could have flown into LAX. But I didn't. I took a deep breath and said, "Yep. It's always like this."

"So how was your day, Coach? Busy day?" He settled in, making small talk as he adjusted the air vent.

Before I could answer, his flip phone began to buzz. He fumbled it to his ear.

"Hello?" he answered.

After a brief moment, he sang with the familiar cadence and tone he uses when giving speeches, or in this case talking to what I assumed was a reporter.

"Bubba was definitely a game changer as a defensive end. You didn't see guys with his size and quickness coming off the defensive line," he trailed.

Isn't it enough that his childhood friend just died? Now he has to take calls from reporters about it? I thought, daydreaming my way through the slow crawl as the smoggy LA skyline came into view. His football career was over before I was born, but moments like these were always a reminder of his celebrity. And that of his friends. My dad retired from 3M Corporation after a long career as a pioneer in diversity recruiting at the end of 2010, on the heels of being named one of the 50 Greatest Minnesota Vikings of all time. His business colleagues and even some of his famous former teammates, like Minnesota supreme court justice

Alan Page (defensive tackle) and former UC Berkeley head football coach Joe Kapp (quarterback), gave their remarks at one of his two epic retirement parties.

I learned so much that I hadn't known about my dad through the speakers who took the podium. It took 11 people to replace him in his role at 3M and about 20 to cover all the different aspects of his professional life in sports, business, and community service in each retirement party program. My favorite moments were when countless mentees and protégés expressed the ways that my dad impacted their careers and lives: *I got my first job, I got a PhD*, and even, *I met my future spouse—because of Gene Washington*.

Admittedly, it was hard not to ear dip in his conversation with the reporter.

"Every school around the country wanted Bubba. They were all trying to recruit him. He and his father put in a good word for me to go to Michigan State. Without that I never would have made it because of the segregation," he concluded, wrapping up the interview from my passenger seat.

He finished the call just as we exited onto La Cienega. We drove deeper into South LA and past a familiar Target store on La Cienega and Rodeo.

"Bubba lived over here, Dad? Do you know how many times I've cut through Baldwin Hills to get to USC to avoid traffic? I could have been walking through the Target parking lot as he passed in his car on the way home and I didn't even know it . . . ," I stammered in disbelief as we pulled up to Bubba's unassuming home.

It had only been a week since Bubba took his last breath. The news teams and their live shots were no longer on the front lawn, as they'd been days earlier. As we entered the home, we were greeted by an overwhelming swell of hugs, *hi theres*, and *You don't remember me, do you? I haven't seen you since you were a little girl, Maya*—pleasantries from former teammates and their still-look-great-for-their-age spouses. There was a quaint little potluck spread of fruit, crackers, cheese, and meats on the dining room table. I politely gnawed on crudités as I took in the space—the home where he died.

It was hard to relax into the rooms where, days prior, Bubba Smith was watching TV or having breakfast. The den reminded me of my dad's trophy room and the '80s, when I'd spread my Barbie Dolls out on the floor surrounded by Gene Washington football memorabilia on every wall. Framed newspaper articles and photographs tiled the wood paneling on Bubba's walls like a dossier, sort of like something you'd see at a celebrity steak house on an episode of *Magnum, P.I.* or *Murder, She Wrote*. Bubba was my first real-life movie star and the only man I'd ever met who was physically bigger than my dad. Sure, I'd met a bunch of football players in my childhood, but my dad's pro career ended long before I was born. Knowing my dad had a friend who was in the *Police Academy* films and on TV commercials was both exciting and extremely bizarre to me. Anytime someone Black was on our TV, growing up in suburban Minneapolis, it was a big deal. When my dad *knew* the Black person on our TV, it was an even bigger deal. Looking at Bubba's walls, it was hard to imagine he and my quiet, reserved dad were friends. Homies. The *for life* kind.

Throughout most of my childhood, my dad was still a public figure in the Twin Cities business arena, where I'd be his plus-one for corporate dinners when my mom traveled and he couldn't find a babysitter. I'm pretty sure that I mastered the handshake, smile, nod, interjection of an affirmative "wow" or "interesting," with a second head nod or raised brow, to demonstrate interest in whatever the adults around us felt like talking about, by the time I was ten years old. I learned it from watching my mom do it, and my older sisters too. We were sincere in our hospitality, but only as an adult do I realize this is a strange skill for a ten-year-old to possess. As I opened a water bottle at Bubba's dining table, I found myself falling into that childhood muscle memory for social occasions surrounding my father, but this time something was different.

I was taken aback by the liveliness of the home, given that we'd collected ourselves within its walls during a time of mourning. If Bubba had hosted a 66th birthday party, or a team reunion in California, inviting his Spartan or NFL brothers to celebrate with him, it's not likely they'd have all flown in from various parts of the country to attend. Yet, death brought them to his living room, his kitchen, and his den, filling his home with memories and laughter in celebration of the life they shared.

The rituals of death have been somewhat constant in my life, from aunts and uncles, old classmates, and quite often the parents of my friends. I've learned through the years that it's important to show up when someone dies. And I'm old enough to know that showing up includes being there for your parents when their friends die too. At least it was occurring to me how important it truly was to share that time with my dad. I was there out of duty as his chauffeur, and perhaps also as a little girl searching for pieces of herself in a dead man's home. As I lost myself in the stream of introductions and stories, I succumbed to the idea that my dad had an actual life, a really *fascinating* life, before I was born.

"Yeah, Maya. They called us the 'Wonder Boys.' I had to come all the way from Beaufort, North Carolina, to become one of the 'Wonder Boys.'" My dad's friend and teammate Ernie Pasteur cracked himself up with a wide smile, holding court in a doorframe, looking like joy with teeth.

"Because you lived in Wonders Hall?" chimed a tall white woman named Marcia, Bubba's college sweetheart, who coordinated the evening. "I remember all of you football players." She shook her head with a knowing smirk. "The 'Wonder Boys.' Is *that* what they called you?"

The room filled with reminiscent laughter. I sat on Bubba's enormous sofa, all five foot two of me, as if I were Lily Tomlin, legs dangling as her comedy character Edith Ann. As if I were the little girl standing next to Bubba while he signed autographs at homecoming or hearing the iconic melody line, "On the banks of the Red Cedar," from the MSU fight song, erupt from the marching band for the first time. I was in heaven listening to stories I'd never heard before.

My dad joined the conversation with details about how he and Bubba played against each other as teenagers in an all-Black league: "Bubba's father was the coach at Charlton-Pollard. Now that's in Beaumont. Way out there in *Beaumont*. They told Duffy about me, 'cause everything was segregated. Michigan State never would have found me if it weren't for him and his father."

Clinton Jones, his Vikings and MSU teammate, burst out in laughter. "Yeah, Gene, it still makes me laugh thinking about how country you were when we came to Michigan State."

"La Porte was small, Clint. The campus was bigger than my hometown," my dad replied with a laugh and a slap to Clinton's back.

I marveled at the string of pearls that make up my dad's smile as he joked with his friends. I live for his smile and the way he moves his arms and spreads out his hands for emphasis. He's rarely that animated, so I enjoyed every minute of it.

Most of my life, I believed magical white men came down to Texas, plucked my dad out of Jim Crow, and gave him a scholarship to MSU. I'd never considered how completely improbable that was, or even how they found La Porte, Texas, on the map. He played for the Vikings, got injured, was traded to the Broncos, retired, and eventually had me. Those were pretty much all the details I knew. It never occurred to either of us that I was missing significant details or context for his athletic career. What good are details in a *Negro makes good* narrative anyway? All people ever wanted to know was if he still goes to all the games and if I could get them an autograph. No one ever asked about the hardships he faced as a Black athlete coming of age during segregation.

I don't know how to see *Gene Washington* as anything but my dad. My hardworking Black dad who kept a roof over my head, made sure I got an education, then framed my degrees and hung them on the wall next to his, my mom's, *and* my sisters' degrees. Simply knowing that a scholarship changed his life, but not much else about his past, had been enough for me. That night, though, it felt as if a desire to know him more fully was awakened. It filled me with both curiosity and shame at the same time. So many people grow up without a dad, or with one who was barely there. *How dare I expect or want more than what I have?*

We headed outdoors to take pictures on Bubba's patio. It was perfect LA weather. With the pool catching moonlight and the occasional fly, it felt more like a barbecue than a wake. I managed the various cell phones passed to me as we tried to get everyone into a group shot.

They were a bunch of people in their 60s, but I could almost imagine them as 20-year-olds. They reminded me of my USC homecoming reunions, reconnecting with old classmates and meeting their spouses and kids. Looking at their faces and my dad's bright smile, it sunk in, really sunk in, that Bubba Smith was the reason that my dad got to Michigan State. The reason my sisters and I had a life my grandparents could never have dreamed of. That moment, like so much of life, was precious. The people who loved Bubba, really *loved* him, posing together in the shadow of their youth, to commemorate the evening, knowing their friend big Bubb—number 95—would be eulogized the following morning.

As we headed back indoors, Bubba's friend Eli, who'd been staying at his house when he died, told me Bubba was trying some new treatments as he recovered from back surgery. They were getting ready to go to the gym, and Eli noticed he'd been in the bathroom a little longer than usual. He discovered Bubba had collapsed on the floor. Up to that point all I'd heard was whatever the news outlets reported. Or speculated. To hear it from Eli knocked all the wind out of my sails. The idea that Bubba hadn't planned to die that day—the fact that it happened while he was in there getting ready to leave home—gutted me.

As the night wore on, nature called me to the bathroom, Eli's story still fresh in my mind and my racing heart. Alone for the first time in a couple of hours, I gave the tears welling in my eyes permission to fall. I dried my hands on Bubba's monogrammed hand towel and whispered *thank you*. There was something about being in the room where he surrendered his spirit. Or at least I believed it was *the* bathroom Eli was referring to. Even if I shed a few tears in the wrong bathroom, the fact that I'd never had an opportunity to thank Bubba personally over-whelmed me. I never had a chance to tell him what a difference he'd made in my dad's life. In *my* life. All because he and his father told the coaches at Michigan State about my dad.

My earliest and most specific memory of Bubba was as a kinder-gartner at homecoming in the '80s, because we have a picture of it. My oldest sister, Lisa, with her Kodak Instamatic camera, advanced her film roll with a click of her thumb and told me to *go stand by Bubba*. So I did. Then I proceeded to live my entire life not knowing that Bubba was a catalyst for the events that changed the trajectory of my family—and history itself. Standing in Bubba's bathroom all those years later was a strange and absolute confrontation. I pondered how my life in LA might have been different if I'd gotten to know Bubba. From all the stories, I'm certain I would have liked him. He probably would have invited me to work out at the gym or attend Bible study. And I probably would have gone, then called my dad to tell him all about it, and weeks later asked him to help me get out of going to both the gym and Bubba's Bible study. Now it's too late for all that.

As we said our goodbyes and headed back to my Corolla, I realized there are things about my dad that I never considered I might *want* to know. There were invitations unsent, or at least unopened, between us. My dad nodded off a bit as I drove us home to my apartment for the night. I was relieved that traffic had died down. As we approached the exit, I thought to myself, *If only figuring out how to have more of this—whatever this time with my dad is—was as clear as the 405 right now.*

CHAPTER

TWO

If the early bird gets the worm, my dad was the dutiful rooster clanking dishes or running the vacuum cleaner first thing in the morning when I was growing up. On this particular morning, we met up in East Lansing, Michigan, so there weren't any chores that day, but an 8:00 a.m. tour of the MSU campus. It felt like the crack of dawn even though the sun had been up a couple of hours. A little extra sleep would have been heavenly, but I was a tad more interested in football after meeting my dad's teammates at Bubba Smith's memorial service months earlier, in August 2011. I found my way into a sweater, jeans, and overcoat suitable for an early October morning. My dad arranged for a tour of the Duffy Daugherty Building and Skandalaris Football Center at Michigan State with one of the last living coaches of his era, defensive coach Henry "Hank" Bullough. As he walked us through every nook and cranny of the building, I instantly took to his gruff yet highly animated vibe. It was clear that Hank Bullough adored my dad and loved Michigan State University.

It was nothing like what my dad's head coach, Duffy Daugherty, the namesake of the building, had in his toolbox to woo potential recruits in the late 1950s and 1960s. It was part museum, part recruitment tool, or recruitment *drool*, really—mainly because of its scope and the very

impressive collection of trophies and NFL helmets representing the
teams where MSU football alumni have made names for themselves and
the university. The interior design was like something out of a modern
luxury architectural magazine, with floor-to-ceiling murals of the program's most accomplished teams, players, and coaches, including a large
section of wall dedicated to my dad and his fellow All-Americans, Bob
Apisa, Clinton Jones, George "Mickey" Webster, and Bubba Smith, in
an iconic photo of them surrounding Duffy Daugherty on the field in
Spartan Stadium. I remembered seeing a few pictures on the wall and a
special plaque for my dad's membership in the MSU Athletics Hall of
Fame back when we visited campus in the 1990s, but this new expansion
had my eyes popping out of my head.

The day was set to be the most significant day in my dad's Spartan
career. The East Lansing reveal of my father's name and jersey number
added to the Ring of Fame in Spartan Stadium was the first of a series of
events that were part of the fanfare that came with being inducted into
the College Football Hall of Fame. Bubba Smith and George Webster
were the only other teammates to share this honor back in 2011, so it
was a *really* big day.

So big that my dad invited his former co-worker from 3M, James
Montague, along with his wife and two young sons, Tré and Jamie, to
share the weekend with us. My mother stayed behind with James's wife,
Renée, at the campus hotel so they could visit with some friends. It was
just me and the guys walking through the building that morning, taking
pictures in front of everything. James's son Tré held my dad's hand as
we meandered through the atrium. It was like watching a stallion walk
a baby chick. Cute stuff. My dad has three daughters and no sons, so
it was a delight to see him walking around hand in hand with a little
Black boy, showing him the different exhibits and enormous trophies.

Hank Bullough was more or less the godfather of MSU football and
quite a seasoned tour guide. He talked with his hands and knew everything about *everything*, which I found endearing. He told us the history

of the building: when they expanded the Duffy Daugherty wing, when they installed the floors, when they upgraded the practice field, and also what hours the study rooms were open to players. He even pointed out a portrait of his grandson Max, who was on the team. The Bullough family is as close to college and pro-football royalty as they come. Hank and his sons played at Michigan State, and within a few short years, there would be three Bulloughs on the team at the same time: Max, Riley, and Byron. Hank went on to coach in the NFL during the late '70s and '80s, and spent most of his retired years being as emblematic of Michigan State football as Sparty, the school's mascot.

"You want to try on my Super Bowl ring?" Hank offered to James's sons.

Tré's eyes widened as he looked to James for permission.

"Go ahead, Tré," James nudged with a smile.

Tré approached Hank slowly as he slid the ring off his finger and put it in Tré's hand. It swung around his little finger like a fat Hula-Hoop encrusted with diamonds.

"Hold it up to your face so your dad can take a picture."

Hank held the ring up to Tré's face and James snapped a shot on his cell phone. His other son, Jamie, took a turn with the impressive hunk of metal. Fear of missing out stirred in me as I watched two little boys live out a dream that I'd never dreamed for myself.

"Can I try it on?" I asked.

"Yeah. You can try it." Hank shrugged, handing the ring to me.

It didn't fit me any better than it did Tré's or Jamie's tiny fingers. I noted the weight of it on my ring finger and this glimpse into the American phenomenon that is gridiron football. There is only a fixed number of Super Bowl rings that exist in the world, and a fixed number of people who've ever tried one on. I can say now that I'm one of them. My whole life is filled with these little moments and memories and perhaps a little embarrassment that I knew so little about the game, or that my dad's NFL Championship ring was even more unique than the enduring symbol of Americana on my ring finger that morning. I removed the ring and handed it back to Coach Bullough. After trying it on, and seeing my dad hand in hand with Tré, and later Jamie, it occurred to me that my dad never officially sat me down and explained the game when I was a kid. Football, track, baseball, basketball, and even golf were always on the TV, but my dad never took the time (that I imagine dads take with sons) to share his love of sports with me.

My glance returned to him as he pointed out different plaques and explained them to James, Jamie, and Tré as we maneuvered through the last bit of the displays. The stats, the figures, and all of the special designations of All-America, Academic All-America, and conference honors more or less went over my head. Nevertheless, I was sincerely impressed with every plaque and certificate on the wall, and the magic of having worn a bona fide Super Bowl ring in the midst of it. There would be a lot of catching up to do if I wanted to fully absorb the football education that I missed when I was Tré's or Jamie's age. As much as I wanted to *lean in* to all the football stuff like the corporate feminists on their national book tours told me I'm supposed to in a so-called man's world, I hadn't had enough caffeine, and my stomach was starting its own rendition of the MSU fight song because I'd skipped breakfast. *Baby steps,* I thought.

We moved outdoors and over to Spartan Stadium. It was homecoming versus Wisconsin, and the parking lot and lawn were filled with tailgaters of all ages. The Spartan Marching Band's explosive rhythms seemed to stir the trees and the winding sidewalks enough to rumble the giant concrete and steel walls of the stadium as we approached on foot. There was an electricity in the air that was different than anything I'd ever experienced. Even more electric than at USC, where I completed my bachelor's degree. I had little personal experience with football games at USC to compare the two schools, but there was an anticipation running through my body that I'd never felt at a college football game anywhere. It might have been the fanfare of my dad's name being added to the Ring of Fame or the fact that we were sharing this moment together and I was old enough to appreciate the legacy I'd unwittingly inherited.

My mom and I watched the festivities and filled our bellies in a suite on the press level of the stadium. It was a little more my speed. *Less people. Less noise. And praise the Lord . . . food.* I positioned myself closer to the glass so that I could make out my dad down on the field waving to the crowd. I was filled with a strange pride when my dad was presented with a plaque from the National Football Foundation and a framed Michigan State Spartans jersey with his embroidered name and number, 84, on the field at halftime. Up toward the top tier of seats, my dad's name and jersey number had been added to the Ring of Fame the night before. Both will live up in the rafters next to Duffy Daugherty, and his teammates Bubba Smith and George Webster, indefinitely— possibly long after he leaves the earth. I was irreversibly intrigued by who my dad was and committed to unearthing the history-altering events that took place in Spartan Stadium.

By the fourth quarter of the game, I was thoroughly invested. The Spartans held a steady lead throughout the game, but Wisconsin tied things up 31–31 with less than a minute and a half left. The entire guest suite held its collective breath. My mother clasped her crimson gel manicure in prayer next to me. I imagined my dad was down on the sideline somewhere with his arms folded and one of his giant hands over his mouth as he watched Spartan quarterback Kirk Cousins complete a few passes, moving the ball to the Wisconsin 44-yard line. With 10 seconds to go, the Spartans called a time-out.

My mother is religious, but also polite. Since we weren't the only people in the suite, she curled her face into her praying hands and began muttering to herself like a squirrel nibbling an acorn. Once play resumed, she lowered herself to the floor and onto her knees as if the kneeling position would be more effective in getting the Lord's attention. I was surprised that it hadn't gotten any of the other people in the suite's attention when the breathy muttering became full-on tongues as if it were Pentecost. She's a tiny little woman, but Claudith Washington holds a lot of religion in a five-foot frame.

Before I could interrupt her personal revival, Kirk Cousins threw an incomplete pass, broken up by Wisconsin's Aaron Henry. It felt like my heart and parts of my soul were twisted into a knot at the base of my stomach. When Wisconsin called a time-out with four seconds left, it felt like complete and utter abuse. It felt like I wasn't even breathing. My mom's verbal genuflection became a bit softer, but she'd planted herself solidly on her knees in front of the glass, and *like a tree planted by the water*, she would not be moved. On the final play, Kirk Cousins launched a Hail Mary pass to Keith Nichol for a 44-yard touchdown. In a matter of seconds, the Spartans won the game 37–31. The entire suite became an explosion of cheers. I helped my mom off the floor, as she jumped around like a giddy child. I'm not sure what happened to me in that moment but I liked it. I *really* liked it.

CHAPTER
THREE

It's not that I didn't like football growing up. It wasn't part of the day-to-day of my childhood like it was for my sisters when my dad was playing for the Vikings. My parents' generation delivered on the future that Dr. Martin Luther King Jr. envisioned in his address at the Youth March for Integrated Schools in 1959 when he said, "I cannot help thinking—that a hundred years from now the historians will be calling this not the 'beat' generation, but the generation of integration."

Football and the backdrop of sweeping civil rights legislation were the vehicles that made it possible for my sisters and me to live an integrated life of access and opportunity—in stark contrast to my parents' childhood experiences. As a small child, I didn't even know what the word "integration" meant, yet I'd lived it since birth. My grandparents made a living working in white homes, but my parents employed a white woman named Aggie to take care of me in theirs. I called her "Grandma Aggie" and never contemplated the optics or genetic impossibilities of a white woman, who was enamored with the Reagans whenever they came on TV, being my *actual* grandmother. Our life was so incredibly integrated that prior to first grade I didn't contemplate my race or anyone else's. This was likely because of the diversity of people that surrounded us.

Instead of your typical American preschool, I attended a Montessori in South Minneapolis. The school was established by the Dairkee family, who were Indian immigrants living in Karachi, Pakistan, before arriving in the US. Some days I'd go home with the school director, Mrs. Dairkee, and play Matchbox cars with her grandson Gabe and other children from school until our parents could pick us up. Her home was as beautiful and tidy as the saris she wore. I mainly remember her sequin-embellished textiles from India, and various folk artworks accented with brass and other metals. Her warm smile enveloped me every morning in the same way that the smoky spices of her cooking and body products scented her hugs.

I looked forward to school every day. Her warmth instilled a wonder and hunger within me to learn and explore. Our classmates came from a variety of backgrounds as well. My best friend was a Jewish girl named Jessica, and Gabe's best friend was a blond boy named Matthew. Gabe, Matthew, and I would act out the characters from the comic books and animated series *Spider-Man and His Amazing Friends*. The boys would take turns as Spider-Man and Iceman, and I was always Firestar by default.

The other kids at school were pretty much a rainbow coalition of races and backgrounds, with some international families thrown in the mix. We'd start our day cross-legged in a circle on the floor. If it was a special day, like someone's birthday, Mrs. Dairkee had a ritual that taught us about astronomy and celebrated our birth in one swoop. On my fifth birthday, I remember holding a small globe of the world that fit in my little hands. Mrs. Dairkee lit a candle on a table in the center of the circle and I walked around it five times, to articulate how many times the Earth traveled around the Sun to mark the anniversary of my birth.

Our multicultural world was a precious one, but occasionally the influences of the terrain outside our little bubble seeped in. One morning during free time, a Native American child who was new to the school singled me out and called me a *nigger*. I'd never heard the word before, but the way he said it gave me the sense that it was not a nice word.

One of the white teaching assistants challenged him aggressively. "Do you know what that word means?"

The boy shrugged. I stood there frozen as the white woman came to my defense.

"It means a person who's not a person. *Maya's* a *person*. So you can't call her that word."

Nothing more was done or said about the incident. I don't think I told my parents, and the staff likely didn't tell them either. As far as I knew, Sunshine Montessori was a happy place where the teachers have your back when kids call you names you've never heard before. Even happier were my car rides with my dad to and from Sunshine Montessori on his daily commute, while my mother and older sisters had their own routine. Every morning he'd help me dress and brush my teeth after he fixed my fine, frizzy hair. I enjoyed the long early morning rides from the western suburbs to Sunshine Montessori, strapped into the leather seats of his silver Mercedes. At the end of the day, he'd pick me up from school just as the janitorial staff started to bring out the brooms and vacuum cleaners. I loved being the first to arrive at Sunshine in the mornings, but I hated being the last kid picked up at night. The late days coincided with the times when he brought me a Twinkie or one of those old-fashioned suckers the size of the giant super balls we'd get in the drugstore vending machines.

My dad and I have always had the ability to keep a comfortable silence between us on car rides. To this day, we don't spend a lot of time chatting the road away, but we have an unspoken agreement between us that sort of asserts that all is well in the world. The drive home from the Montessori sometimes took us around Minneapolis's Chain of Lakes, including Lake Harriet and Lake Calhoun (whose name was recently restored to its original Dakota name, Bde Maka Ska). He'd listen to country radio and cassette tapes of the Commodores and Stevie

Wonder, singing along for every other phrase. As we'd meander through neighborhood streets and eventually the freeway, the electric poles were familiar friends moving toward the window like faithful guides lining our way home.

Since my sisters were significantly older than me, I was his tagalong kid on weekends when he went to get gas for the lawnmower or make a run to the hardware store. Monday through Friday he'd wear business suits, but on weekends he'd rock a white T-shirt and tomato-red BIKE brand athletic shorts, with tall white socks and loafers. His legs were so long his knees rested on either side of the steering column. My favorite errands were visits to the Wayzata Bay Center where he'd get his suits tailored at the Foursome department store. Bridgeman's Ice Cream Shoppe was in the same complex, and I often scored a scoop of Peppermint Bon Bon at the end of the trip, if I played my cards right. People were kind and attentive to my dad everywhere we went. He'd smile and wave at everyone, and I recall often asking him, "How do you know these people?"

He'd say, "I don't. They're just being friendly."

People were always friendly. I don't think I truly had a sense of how famous he was when he played for the Vikings or how many people still recognized him in the '80s. In hindsight I now realize that people in the community *knew* he was Gene *Washington* and treated him and the rest of our family well because of it.

When first grade arrived, my parents enrolled me in the public elementary school in our neighborhood. It meant that, at six years old, I didn't have any more long car rides with Dad and I wouldn't see Mrs. Dairkee or my Montessori friends every day. Fortunately, I received a warm welcome from the teacher, Mrs. Petty, but went from being one of a handful of brown and tan kids to being the only Black child in the entire first grade, and one of three in the entire school.

I was an early reader thanks to Mrs. Dairkee, but my spelling needed work. In the first few weeks of school, I'd sign my work phonetically,

Maya *Washeenten,* at the top of my papers. I was quickly sent to the school language specialist so I could learn how to properly spell my last name. In those days my parents' main objective was to keep us alive while they worked long hours in corporate America. They weren't extremely involved in my classroom exploits as a first grader, and barely managed to sign permission slips or keep up with whatever notices were sent home. Teaching me how to spell my government name sort of slipped through the cracks.

Over the weekend, my mom spent some time committing each letter of *Maya Thérèse Washington* to my memory at the kitchen table while my dad watched football. I was so proud and excited to show off for the language specialist when I returned to class on Monday. I hoped she'd be impressed enough to release me from our little meetings that took place during my favorite hour of the day, reading. I'd barely tucked my tongue back inside my mouth, concentrating on the extra-wide-ruled paper with my No. 2 pencil, before she took a fat pink eraser and raked it over the accents in my middle name. She pressed so hard it ripped the paper. I was stunned and confused as she tore through me and every *Marie Thérèse* in my Creole bloodline, leaving a rubber dust trail as if my heritage were a foreign object that needed to be removed.

I was quickly adopted by three blonde girls in my class, Sarah, Lissa, and Kirsi, who'd attended kindergarten at the school. They were sweet but weird, petting my hair and skin and remarking how soft they were. We pledged allegiance to the flag of the United States of America every morning. In November we made paper cutouts of "Pilgrims and Indians" and attached their limbs with brass brads so we could pose and move them. We used crayons to color in their buckskin clothing, shiny gold buckles, headdresses, and Pilgrim hats. In typical fashion, we never discussed genocide or colonization.

In January, my parents took us out of school on Martin Luther King Jr.'s birthday. The day wasn't a holiday yet, but it was a stance they took every year to acknowledge their Black children's place in an all-white school district. We'd attend an early morning breakfast in the Black community where we'd sing the Black National Anthem, "Lift Every Voice and Sing," and hear speeches from civic leaders.

I'm not sure if it was a regularly scheduled lesson or the result of my absence on January 15, but sweet, white Mrs. Petty rolled out the media cart, and we watched an old black-and-white film showing Black people being hosed down and attacked by dogs in Birmingham, Alabama, in 1963. I don't recall her offering any context for Black people being brutalized by high-pressure water hoses or the gnashing teeth of the police dogs. I also don't recall my parents introducing me to the civil rights movement as events they'd actually lived through. I slowly became more aware of racial differences—how my school friends had white Barbie Dolls, and I had Black ones (when we were able to find them). I had white friends at school, and Black, brown, and other friends on the weekends.

On Sundays we'd attend Saint Joan of Arc Catholic Church in Minneapolis as a family. I spent Mass in the childcare room playing with kids of every race. It was a real hippie church led by Father Harvey Egan, who looked a lot like Willie Nelson to me. They had guitars and amps and projected the song lyrics on a giant screen next to the altar, which was positioned at one end of the school gymnasium. Often the Communion and closing hymns might be a secular song like "Shower the People" or "You've Got a Friend" performed in the style of Carole King and James Taylor. Our world was always diverse and mostly intersectional in our understanding of *loving your neighbor as yourself*, but very much compartmentalized geographically between Minneapolis and the western suburbs.

My parents demonstrated the importance of Blackness and Black community in how we moved in the world. When we'd see a Black face at the grocery store or the mall near our home, my parents would take the time to introduce themselves and welcome them to the community. We always had extra guests at Thanksgiving and Christmas, and planned social gatherings with Black and brown families. If someone

Black came on TV, my mom would yell for all of us to "come, quick! They've got a Black girl on the news tonight."

My parents volunteered for the United Negro College Fund telethons and supported the Twin Cities television broadcast of Lou Rawls's *An Evening of Stars* from a local station. I even got to go on air in the wee hours of the night in second grade to deliver the slogan, *A mind is a terrible thing to waste.* I was trembling with nerves in my white lace First Communion dress as I allowed each syllable to escape my lips. Within the hour, the announcer, Greg Coleman, also a former Minnesota Viking, commented on how my on-air moment helped them get more pledges.

Participating in community activities with my family was one of my favorite things in the whole wide world. My sisters were often invited to Jack and Jill social events with other Black teenagers from all around the Twin Cities. I enjoyed watching them get ready for dances and dates with Black boys from other parts of town. There was stability in being Gene and Claudith's daughter, and Lisa and Gina's little sister. We had a sense of sanctuary in the Black community that gave me the sense that I belonged to something, even though I didn't fully understand why I'd never truly belong in the white community where we lived.

Years later, I appreciate every hand my father shook, and every door he pried open for himself and countless others in his work as a human resources professional. Whether it was bringing me a piece of candy, a key chain, an embroidered golf shirt, or a little lapel pin he got at a conference when he'd return from a business trip, my dad dutifully presented me with the artifacts of what he was building for our family and for other families in America. The trinkets were rarely extravagant, but they signaled that any time he had to leave home, he would always come back.

When he wasn't traveling, I liked spending time with him. Sure, he made me pull weeds for hours in the summer, but he took me to the Vikings' annual toy giveaway every winter. Every Christmas Eve we'd spend the whole morning and afternoon distributing toys to families who couldn't manage extra luxuries during the holidays. A room in a community center in Minneapolis was transformed and stacked floor to ceiling with games, books, trucks, dolls, and other toys for all ages. It was like a pop-up soup kitchen for toys. As an adult, I realize those families probably would have appreciated *actual* soup—or a whole meal, toiletries, and warm clothes—even more than the toys, but as a child I drank and served the charity Kool-Aid with my whole heart. There was likely food at the event, but all I remember is the room full of toys.

While my dad and other Vikings alumni would work the line, the other players' kids and I would run to the back to pick out a toy suited for the ages of the children written on a slip that the parents would provide. It was a dream to be surrounded by so many toys. I put a lot of thought into picking out the right gift for each child on the list.

We participated in a lot of charitable events but rarely went to any Vikings games, if ever. Year-round sports were always on TV in the background as my dad worked late at night, preparing for presentations or conferences in the den that also served as his trophy room. I'd occasionally be invited to Twins baseball games with my school friends' families, and I thought it was cool that my dad's friend Rod Carew used to play with the team.

For one of my dad's birthdays, my mother commissioned a funny illustration of a man who seemed to be passed out on his desk at work after eating too much popcorn. It was the perfect gift because my dad had a ritual of popping kernels on the stove once a week in a giant gumbo pot. He'd shake the mess out of that pot as each little kernel exploded against the stainless steel, then dump the tremendous mound of popcorn onto the countertop, paper towels catching each perfectly popped bit. The smell and sound of Dad's popcorn popping would bring our house full of women into the kitchen, to fill our palms with handfuls while it was still hot.

Throughout the week, he'd eat what was left of the popcorn out of a giant Tupperware container while he watched sports. I was never formally invited to watch with him, but I remember we at least shared an affinity for Black women who were Olympic athletes, such as Debi Thomas, Florence Griffith Joyner, and Jacqueline Joyner-Kersee. And years later, the 1992 USA Olympic men's basketball "Dream Team." Magic Johnson (a fellow Spartan) and Michael Jordan were rock stars to me. Other than that, professional sports were always part of my peripheral experience of my dad hanging out in his den, but not a pastime that we shared.

While my mom and sisters were busy shopping or participating in middle and high school activities, I was forced to accompany my dad to the YMCA, where he'd play pickup basketball with men his age, and sometimes the teenage boys my sisters went to school with. It was a rowdy vibe, with a lot of sneaker squeaks and funky sweat, as far as I was concerned. Still, it was better than following my mom and sisters around the mall. I often wandered the building and watched the swimmers doing laps in the pool from the observation deck window, remembering the days when he'd taught me how to swim when I was a toddler. I'd walk around the running track out of boredom, then eventually kick it by the vending machines with the money he gave me to buy snacks.

I attended high school basketball games occasionally because my oldest sister, Lisa, was the statistician for the Wayzata boys' basketball team. She was my babysitter, so I didn't really have a choice. During the games, I'd play in the bleachers and walk around the gymnasium, oblivious to what was happening on court. Lisa and her teenage life embodied everything good and angsty about a John Hughes film in the '80s, only Black. She and our sister, Gina, loved fashion and pop culture, went to Prince parties and video shoots, and did whatever cool Black girls from the suburbs were into back in those days.

I looked up to both Lisa and Gina because they were everything I thought being a teenager was all about. Gina, my dad's namesake, was more of a bookworm, and the only Black face in the choir and on the sidelines waving her pom-poms at the football, basketball, and hockey games. She was a tiny little thing with a red lip and a thousand-watt smile that refused to quit. Lisa, on the other hand, was my dad's athlete protégé, destined to carry on his legacy in the track world. She had long, strong legs that earned her statewide recognition as a sprinter. Lisa and my dad had a special connection because he took great interest in her track career. They'd train in the early mornings, and he'd record film of her on his Super 8 camera. She ran anchor leg on the 4-by-100-meter relay team with three other Black girls at the school. There were only five other Black families in the Wayzata community for most of my early childhood, and their team represented four of the five, including Lisa.

The victories were sweet, but watching Lisa and my dad butt heads as a kid was exhausting. He trained her like an elite athlete preparing for the Olympics, because at the peak of his career, *he* was that good. And *Lisa* was that good. Sometimes the training sessions were as romantic as the montage scene in *Rocky III*, where Sylvester Stallone trains for the big fight underscored by the rhythmic guitar line of "Eye of the Tiger." Most of the time, though, it was like watching prize fighters duke it out to the death. She often complained and protested, and he'd shout coaching commands back, neither willing to bend to each other's will. The constant tension made it seem like being the *athletic daughter* was a lousy gig. Still, I looked up to both my dad and my big sister and put in my best effort during physical education in elementary school. I only wanted to play wide receiver during the football unit in gym class, and I ran the 100-yard dash in the annual track meet. I had natural athletic ability, but I wasn't so great at catching a football, and I didn't come in first place in anything in co-ed track and field but second, third, and sometimes fifth place. I had my dad's competitive mindset, but the athletic ability would take development that I didn't have the patience for.

In fourth grade, my classmate Suzie invited me to join her softball team in a nearby community called Hamel. It was even more small-town than Plymouth and Wayzata, the developing suburbs where I lived. I feel like Hamel literally had one main street, and the rest of the area was made up of homesteads spread out between farmlands. Softball seemed to be an answer to my dilemma, *How do I do sports—but without my dad making me run laps or take ice baths?* That was until my dad came home with a new glove and a T-ball post. I had no idea my dad had played baseball in high school on a team with adults from his community. Around the time those "Bo Knows" Nike commercials featuring Bo Jackson were running on network television, I quickly learned that Gene Washington also knew, and was damn good at, every sport imaginable.

When he invited me to play catch and practice my swing in the backyard, he critiqued my form, then made me run laps at the park across the street. This was not my idea of "fun time" with Dad. He'd tell me how to hold the bat, what I wasn't doing right, and how I was *supposed to* do it. I sort of zoned out and went through the motions until he wiped his brow, saying, "That's enough for today."

I refused to *practice* outside of practice, so I was mediocre at best when I was up to bat, but I could run bases like no one's business. The coach usually put me in the outfield where the ball never went. Occasionally the big white farm girls we'd play in greater Minnesota would send one out over my head and get a home run. Even if I had put a little more focus into our workouts in the suburbs, in my ten-year-old imagination the rural girls had nothing better to do than hit softballs out into their pastures and cornfields for hours before *and after* school. My contribution to the team wasn't my athletic prowess but in making up cheers from the bench and being the life of the party at Dairy Queen after we slapped the farm girls' winning hands in the high-five parade of "Good game, good game, good game . . ." showing our great sportsmanship after a royal tail whooping.

The thing I didn't enjoy was when we'd stop in the rural towns where the all-white staff and patrons at the Dairy Queen or country diner would stare at me in a way that made the hair in my kitchen, at the nape of my Black neck, stand up. I don't think I'd even learned about Emmett Till or the stories of what happens to Black children when they're assaulted by racist white hostilities at that point in my life. Yet, I knew that being Black in these small white towns was something that made me nervous. I don't know that I thought they'd kill me and dump me in a river, but I knew to be cautious and didn't like the feeling of fear those piercing stares stirred in my body.

I quickly ascribed this feeling of unspecified danger to white people who lived in rural Minnesota. I remember visiting white classmates who lived in rural areas and hearing their family members refer to Brazil nuts as *nigger toes* without flinching around me. By now I knew *nigger* was a bad word. That it meant a Black person. That it meant *me*.

A new kid who was trying to fit in called Suzie from softball and our other friend Sarah *nigger lovers* for hanging out with me at recess. Suzie, Sarah, and all the other kids who'd known me since first grade shut his redheaded, freckle-faced foolishness down. His attempt to make friends via white supremacy fell tremendously flat at Greenwood Elementary. Without the weight of Jim Crow as context or even a sense of the origin story and etymology of a phrase like *nigger lover*, the other kids and I weren't the right audience for his attempt to either fit in or shame us. I kind of felt sorry for him because no one wanted to be his friend before or after he made that comment.

I was mostly treated well by my teachers and classmates. Aside from the occasional insult or slur, I thrived in my school community. I truly enjoyed going to school every day, oblivious to how hard my parents' generation fought for me to have the opportunity to get a public education equal to my white peers'.

Once on a Friday in third grade, I was putting away my folder on the bookshelf while my classmates read independently. The office clerk's voice interrupted the quiet via the classroom intercom: "Please send Maya Washington to the office."

It was an unusual request, most likely met by gasps and *Ooo, you're in trouble* from my classmates while the teacher hushed them. I went down to the office and my dad was standing at the front desk.

"Where's your backpack? We've got to go," he said, hurried.

"What? I can't just leave, Dad! You have to send a note if you take me out."

He shrugged me off, and I went back to class and picked up my stuff. I hopped in the car, pouting to myself. I was so incredibly irritated. *What the hell?* I thought in my *nine-year-old using curse words* mind. *He takes me out of reading class with no warning?* I continued to fume until we pulled up to the University of Minnesota's basketball gymnasium. As we got out of the car, I was completely incredulous. *He's taken me out of school for a BASKETBALL GAME?!*

He bought me a soda and snacks, and I eased into the randomness of it all as the MSU Spartans took on the Minnesota Gophers on their home court. It was a close game. I mostly fixated on the Spartan cheerleaders. I'd never seen a girl balancing on one foot in the palm of a guy's hand. Their strength and athleticism was like watching the high-wire act or the flying trapeze at the circus. I didn't feel as warm about the Gopher cheerleaders though. I couldn't stand how they screamed and shook their pom-poms when the Spartans were at the free-throw line.

"How rude!" I folded my arms in great offense. "How are they supposed to make the shot if they're screaming like that, Dad?"

I had a blast at the game, but I scolded him on the way home. "You have to have a note next time, Dad. You can't just take me out of school like that, okay?"

These little attempts to connect through sports and his Spartans went over my head every time.

CHAPTER
FOUR

The months after Bubba's death lit a fire in my grateful heart, and its embers ignited the soles of my feet to put in the effort to learn more about my dad's time with Bubba at MSU. It's as if my dad and I both started new life chapters at the same time. He was entering retirement, and I was taking on new adventures as an artist. As an actor, I longed to be more engaged in the storytelling process. Dramatic writing and directing gave me an opportunity to bring stories of diversity forward in ways that reignited my passion as an artist during that time. My directorial debut, *White Space*, a narrative short film about a deaf performance poet, was touring internationally, so I caught the proverbial directing bug around the same time my better understanding of Bubba's role in my father's journey out of segregation came to light. The more articles I read and questions I asked, the more I began to understand that Bubba and my dad were part of something so groundbreaking and historic that I was compelled to document it all on film.

A feature-length documentary was a bigger project than I'd ever taken on, but I was up for the challenge. There was grief in the realization that it was too late to thank Bubba Smith for what he and his father did for our family. There was also a part of me that longed to feel closer to my dad through quality time and stories. It was hard not to consider my dad's mortality, and the reality that our time together was limited. The closest example I have for what I longed to share with my dad was the way that my mom's first cousin Benny and I grew close over the years. Whenever I felt lost or unsure of myself in my career or in my life, I could always spill my heart out as I followed Benny around while he tinkered in the garage or the yard. No matter what had me up in arms in any given moment, he listened intently; then when it was clear that I'd gotten it all out, he'd look up at me and say, "Well, you've got a lot of stress. But I know you'll come out on top. I don't care what nobody say. You're all right in my book."

Benny was there with a listening ear, a front-row seat at my performances, or an extra guest room (with a small college portrait of my mother on the night table). I'd even slip and call him *Dad* from time to time. He called me "Maya Maya" and introduced me to his friends and sometimes to strangers as his "Little Girl." I also earned the occasional title of "Secretary," because he'd often ask me to proofread his speeches for his Masonic Lodge and other correspondence to tidy up the side effects of lifelong dyslexia and a mild stroke. During most of my visits, I'd sit at his kitchen counter while he made himself fried bologna or poured himself some coffee. I learned so much about his life while sitting at his kitchen counter: how he met his wife, and how he reconnected with his brothers after his mother died when he was a small boy. Benny possessed the tenderness and vulnerability I'd always longed to experience from my dad. They were two very different men, but they enjoyed a special bond between them—family by marriage, and buddies by choice.

Not only did my dad bring artifacts home from his trips to give me as a kid, but he also left a few at Benny's house. Every visit to Benny's was underscored by the sounds of a little TV set in his kitchen, which swiveled on a lazy Susan. During one of my long weekend visits, Benny told me the story of how my dad bought him the TV on one of his trips to Southern California. In Benny's bathroom there was a "guest book" filled with entries from friends and family who visited over the years. Among my favorite pages is an entry that my dad left after an earthquake interrupted his morning shave when he was staying with Benny during a business trip. I loved to page through to my dad's entry, and the ones I wrote as a child when we visited for the funeral of his wife, Babs, and when I first moved to California to attend college. I spent hours in Benny's home—living and breathing what I imagined a father-daughter relationship was supposed to look like, as the TV my dad bought him was eternally broadcasting ABC7 News, right there with us the whole time.

As I started the research process to bring a documentary to fruition, I realized there was no guarantee that my dad and I would ever be two peas in a pod the way that Benny and I became, but I was willing to make the effort. I hoped that the more I learned, and the more I talked to people connected to my dad's story, the more I'd fill in some of that longing. At a minimum, I'd attempt to fulfill an unshakable desire to share the historical information I'd uncovered with others. As I dove into biographies, news clippings, and ephemera about Duffy Daugherty and the events that unfolded at Michigan State 50 years prior, I was stunned that the history that took place in East Lansing, on the banks of the Red Cedar River, wasn't more widely known.

It's not like my dad's college coach, Duffy Daugherty, just woke up one day and announced to his family on the way home from Mass on Easter Sunday that he was going to desegregate college football. From what I understand, there was no apparition or visit from an archangel or the Blessed Virgin. He didn't look up in the rearview mirror at his adolescent son, Danny, in the back seat and say, *How 'bout we get some Black players on the team?* like something out of a Kevin Costner movie.

It was so gradual that a lot of people missed it, forgot about it, or have no idea how significant Duffy Daugherty and all of the Black men he recruited from the late 1940s to the late 1960s are to understanding how college football became a fully integrated sport. Sports journalists and historians call Duffy Daugherty's pipeline from the segregated South to Michigan State the "Underground Railroad" of College Football, but it wasn't a railroad at all. There was nothing underground about it. It all happened right out in the open for all to see. Invoking the Underground Railroad seems sacrilegious to me when talking about football and not human beings escaping chattel slavery, but the thematic relationship between my dad's generation and our enslaved ancestors is undeniable. For my dad and others, leaving Jim Crow behind for a college education and better opportunity in the North was a form of escape, filled with great risk, mental and physical fortitude, and courage, whether they fully recognized it at the time or not.

Perhaps the epitome of privilege for those of us who are the first generation to live in an integrated world is the way that we take for granted the specifics of the sacrifices and subsequent strides our parents and grandparents made so that we could get our Black lives and be great in the 21st century. Our ancestors were often so focused on survival that they weren't necessarily concerned about making history, but simply making a contribution as they improved their own lives, and subsequently those of future generations. Similarly, my sisters and I weren't thinking, *Look at us, we're integrating an entire school district right now*, when we grew up in an all-white community. We were simply living the life that was laid out before us at the time. We did our best to maneuver in communities that didn't always want us there.

The idea that I was witnessing the progress that my ancestors didn't live to see in the flesh filled my being as I took in the bustling lobby of the Waldorf Astoria in New York for my father's College Football Hall of Fame dinner celebration. Attending my dad's formal induction into the College Football Hall of Fame in December 2011 felt as important to me as showing up for Bubba's funeral a few months prior. With every interview, panel, or event related to his accomplishments, my dad continually remarked that football is a team sport, and anything he was able to achieve on the field was due in large part to his coaches and teammates.

It was a black-tie affair hosted by the National Football Foundation with all of the honorees seated on a dais at the end of the ballroom. I didn't grow up around football players, so thoughts of *Beauty and the Beast* came to mind as I scanned the room full of broad-shouldered men in tuxes accompanied by their teeny tiny dates in evening gowns.

The induction event was like the Kennedy Center Honors for college football players—at least that's my best comparison to the arts world, anyway. My mother, my sister Lisa, and I were seated at the Michigan State table, where I had a chance to thank quarterback Kirk Cousins personally for the Hail Mary pass at the homecoming game since he was also being honored with the Big Ten Sportsmanship Award. It's probably the first and only time I've ever complimented a football player on a specific play in that way that literary or performing artists reflect on the nuance of a specific line or dramatic device when complimenting one another's work. Instead of the obligatory social scripts I'd grown accustomed to enduring at many a corporate banquet or wedding in my lifetime, I found myself genuinely interested in what Kirk and his father, who accompanied him to dinner, had to say as the salad dressing made its way around the table.

Seeing my dad introduced, then watching him take his place on the dais, was similar to the thrill I feel when one of my nieces is up on stage for a school play or violin concert. As a smile spread across my face, Becky Dantonio, former MSU head coach Mark Dantonio's wife, put a loving hand on my shoulder as the room rumbled applause. Becky was everything you'd expect a Becky to be—blonde and beautiful in an evening gown. Beyond the cliché, I found a deep inner strength and power grounded in authenticity and warmth. Becky's friendly energy put me at ease, which I desperately needed because just before we took our seats, my mother critiqued the way I'd talked with my hands during the reception, earlier in the evening. Never mind that I'm a grown-ass woman; my mom can still cut me in half with a look or unsolicited and incidental feedback.

I'm certain there's a special place in heaven for football wives and the social responsibilities that come with living life under the gaze of the public's eye. There are things that I will never understand about my mother or the journey she inadvertently took alongside my dad for years. I've probably learned more about both of their lives from public speeches than I have from intimate conversations in private. Among the standout, go-to one-liners my dad offers when giving speeches is an all-time crowd pleaser: "Claudith and I were bused to the same school in ninth grade. I can say that at least one good thing came out of segregation. We've been married 54 years."

My mom always smiles graciously in the midst of the admiring sighs of the crowd, then whispers to me, "He always says that, and we weren't even dating back then. We were just friends until college."

If I'm lucky there will also be a special place in heaven for the children of football wives. Amazingly, throughout the College Football Hall of Fame dinner, I found myself able to escape the pins and needles that sometimes accompanied being Gene and Claudith Washington's daughter, and settled into the awe I felt in my actual human *being*—that my dad was forever enshrined in American football history. Seeing my dad on the dais with the other inductees further nudged the seed that Bubba's death had planted in my heart months earlier. Bubba's memorial service, the Spartan Ring of Fame, and the College Football Hall of Fame induction event provided a platform to talk about his experiences during segregation publicly in a way I'd never heard before.

~

To understand where my dad, Bubba, and their teammates fit into the desegregation of college football, it's important to note that a series of events occurred almost 100 years before they were born that made a pipeline from Texas segregation to Michigan State possible. Their alma mater started as a land-grant institution called the Agricultural College of the State of Michigan in 1855. The simple college pretty much looked like a giant farm with a handful of buildings. It would be another hundred years before what is now known as Michigan State University could become a football powerhouse.

Around the turn of the 20th century, the institution began enrolling women and a small handful of African American students. Months after a group primarily consisting of white women marched in the Woman Suffrage Procession in Washington, DC, the college started a Black football player, Gideon Smith, in 1913. It had been 50 years since the Emancipation Proclamation, and only a few major institutions in the United States had enrolled a Black player by that time. Only the University of Michigan (George Jewett), the University of Nebraska (George Flippin), Ohio State (Fred Patterson), Indiana University (Preston Eagleson), the University of Iowa (Frank Kinney Holbrook), and the University of Minnesota (Bobby Marshall) had dared to dip a toenail into integrated waters by adding Black players to their rosters from 1890 to Gideon Smith's first game.

Gideon's hopes and the potential for the school to have Black players moving forward were nearly dashed when head coach John Macklin turned him away and refused to issue a team uniform because of the color of his skin. Smith showed up for practice in borrowed gear from another student. This show of determination won Coach Macklin over, and Smith was added to the 1913 varsity roster as a tackle. Gideon Smith was both the first Black football player at the institution and the first Black varsity athlete in the school's history.

As much as these early examples of schools opening their doors to Black players evoke Jackie Robinson-esque themes of perseverance, and white folks willing to breach "the color line" and secure a place on the right side of history, the racial integration of college football was a long process and mirrored the suffering Black people outside of sports faced in the US. In 1923, a Black football player named Jack Trice was given the opportunity to play at Iowa State. Housing discrimination against Black people required that he live off campus with his wife, but the Athletics Department was still willing to give him a shot on the team. It wasn't long before Iowa State received letters from other institutions on their football schedule who refused to play the Cyclones if they started Jack Trice. Missouri, Kansas, and Oklahoma were among those willing to forfeit rather than meet an integrated Iowa State team on the field.

The University of Minnesota was one of the few institutions willing to play Iowa State with a game scheduled for October 6, the second game in the Cyclones' season. When the team arrived in Minneapolis, Jack was not permitted to room with his white teammates or eat in the hotel dining room. Despite the discriminatory treatment he encountered, Jack was filled with pride and an understanding that this game against Minnesota was an important moment for his family and his race. A note that he wrote on the Curtis Hotel's stationery serves as a record of his sense of mission in this powerful moment.

> *My thoughts just before the first real college game of my life: The honor of my race, family and self are at stake. Everyone is expecting me to do big things. I will! My whole body and soul are to be thrown recklessly about on the field tomorrow. Every time the ball is snapped, I will be trying to do more than my part.*
>
> *—Jack*

As the only Black person to step onto the field that Saturday, Jack Trice was determined to achieve the goals he'd set for himself the night before. Within minutes, history took a horrific turn. According to various historical accounts, Jack either broke his collarbone or severely injured his shoulder during the second play in the game but wouldn't take himself out. He persisted in grueling game play until the end of the third quarter when he went for a "roll block," throwing himself onto an opposing player to make a tackle that landed him on his back. Once he was on the ground, three of Minnesota's players stomped him mercilessly as the crowd at Northrop Field watched on. Later as he was carried off in a stretcher, the Gopher fans gave up "We're sorry, Ames!" chants. Jack was taken to a local hospital and released hours later. He boarded the train back to Iowa with his team. He was in excruciating pain and was steadily bleeding internally. That train ride must have felt like an eternity to Jack Trice. He made it back to Ames, but died two days later.

When I first learned about Jack Trice's story, and what the racial climate in the Twin Cities was like at the time, it became palpable how much early Black players sacrificed so that years later my dad and others could break down the barriers their predecessors had been clawing away for half a century. The same year that Jack Trice was trampled within an inch of his life, and later died from those injuries, the University of Minnesota's yearbook featured an image of a Ku Klux Klan float in the homecoming parade, and the local Klan organization put its "Exalted Cyclops" (official title), Roy Miner, up as a Saint Paul mayoral candidate.

The fact that Jack Trice, by today's definition, was the victim of a hate crime, simply for participating in a college football game, forces me to consider the improbability of my dad's recruitment to play Big Ten football 40 years later—or that he'd someday call Minnesota home after playing for the Minnesota Vikings. Based on the Jack Trice tragedy alone, who could have predicted the extent to which the University of Minnesota, or college football itself, would eventually welcome Black athlete participation in Division I competition?

The strangest thing about the events at the University of Minnesota in 1923 was that about 20 years before Jack Trice had been fatally injured on its football field, the school successfully introduced Bobby Marshall, a Black end, to what was then the Big Nine Conference. Marshall was the first person of color to play in the entire conference when he took the field in 1904. He received All-America honors in 1905 and 1906, and was part of two Big Ten Championships for the University of Minnesota. He was the epitome of the success adage, *You have to work twice as hard, and you have to run twice as fast,* that Black American parents spoon-feed to their children before the first tooth pokes out of their gums. In addition to his college football accomplishments, Bobby Marshall graduated with a law degree and earned All-Conference honors in baseball and lettered in track. He even played for a semiprofessional Negro League and was one of the first Black players in the NFL, in addition to playing professional hockey and competing as a professional boxer.

The University of Minnesota's historical relationship with Black athletes illustrates the tensions imbedded in America's struggle with *the race question.* The Big Ten Conference would have to decide whether they'd strive to be a beacon of inclusion or uphold racial segregation like other collegiate conferences around the country. For my dad and other Black athletes of the 1960s, pioneers like Bobby Marshall, Gideon Smith, and their contemporaries paved the way for the next generation despite the ways that the United States wrestled with a shaky moral conscience.

In 1941, after a stint as the secretary of the State Board of Agriculture, John A. Hannah, a boot-strapping 39-year-old white poultry farmer from humble beginnings, became the president of the institution— renamed Michigan State College of Agriculture and Applied Science (MSC) in 1925. Throughout the 1940s, MSC began to mold itself into the perfect setting for a seismic shift that would change college athletics forever. John A. Hannah's tenure as university president led to expansion efforts that transformed MSC into the major research institution (and member of the Big Ten Conference) known since 1964 as Michigan State University (MSU). One of the new president's core beliefs, providing financial support to student athletes, would be among the foundational steps that led to the success of Duffy Daugherty's Underground Railroad of College Football pipeline, and my dad's journey from segregated La Porte, Texas, to integrated East Lansing, Michigan, years later.

President Hannah had a deep appreciation for athletics because he didn't have the opportunity to participate in sports as a child. His family farm was too far away for him to attend practices *and* keep up with his chores. As a young adult, John A. Hannah loved attending college sports, especially football, when he was a student at the University of Michigan, and later when he transferred to MSC to complete a degree in agriculture. His passion for recruiting began when he became friendly with head football coach Jim Crowley and his wife, Helen. Jim Crowley brought a little fame to the institution because he was a well-known Notre Dame football player in his own right and lives in history as one of the Four Horsemen of Notre Dame football alongside three other defensive players photographed on horseback in 1924.

The friendship led to Hannah being an unofficial recruiter in the remote and rural parts of Michigan in hopes that he might persuade promising players to attend MSC. This continued when a new head coach, Charlie Bachman, arrived at the institution in 1933. Since it was in the middle of the Great Depression, all the college could offer talented high school athletes was the chance to attend college. The student athletes of those early years would have to find loans and maybe a part-time job (at 35 cents an hour) to cover their tuition, books, and living expenses in addition to playing football for the school. To offset the financial hardships for students and athletes whose families couldn't help pay expenses, Hannah helped organize a room and board co-op on campus in the basement of Wells Hall. The co-op made meals available for $2.50 a week, in exchange for working in the kitchen and dining room. If students couldn't afford the $2.50 a week, they could provide fresh produce or dairy from their family farms to cover their meals.

Years later, when he became university president in 1941, John A. Hannah set up the Jenison Awards, a financial aid program for student athletes in memory of alumnus Fred C. Jenison. Hannah was the executor of the Jenison estate, which was bequeathed to MSC with the stipulation that funds had to be used for the improvement of the institution. The recipients were held to the same admission standards as other students, expected to be in the top third of their graduating high school classes, and required to take a full load of coursework every academic year. The award further allowed students to continue their education if they weren't able to participate in athletics due to an injury or "lack of ability." It provided tuition and fees, and loaned textbooks to the student athletes in the program.

In many ways this form of financial support is common in college athletics in the 21st century. A lot of American families depend on athletic scholarships to finance their children's college education. My dad wouldn't have had the opportunity to pursue his education at Michigan State without the scholarship he was given. My grandparents couldn't afford to send him to a local Black college, let alone a predominantly white institution like Michigan State.

John A. Hannah's innovation made a significant impact on the growth of the football program. Unfortunately, the Jenison Awards program became a point of contention for MSC's acceptance into what would become the Big Ten Conference. The University of Chicago left the conference in 1946, creating a potential opening for MSC. The Big Nine faculty representatives, consisting of educators from the University of Illinois, Indiana University, the University of Iowa, Ohio State University, Purdue University, the University of Michigan, the University of Minnesota, Northwestern University, and the University of Wisconsin, were reluctant to open their doors to MSC.

Aside from World War II putting a freeze on previous conversations, the main argument for denying MSC's application to replace the University of Chicago was that the faculty members representing the

Council of Nine believed in the philosophical idea of *amateur play* in college athletics, first introduced by the National Collegiate Athletic Association (NCAA) in a code of ethics in 1906. It was a noble and necessary concern at the time, because college football nationwide had become ruthless in its efforts to recruit players. The intention was to rein in *pay-for-play* behavior. The practical application of this code of ethics meant that scholarships, loans, meals, and part-time employment offers were considered forms of pay that were forbidden.

It was an ethical and philosophical stance that continues to plague college athletics in the 21st century. The question of compensating student athletes for the grueling commitment to their sport and their academic studies while being logistically limited in their ability to gain part-time employment to apply to additional expenses (toiletries, school supplies, family responsibilities, transportation, clothing, entertainment, etc.) not covered by their scholarships is still heavily debated in American culture today. The NCAA of 1906 could never have imagined the amount of revenue that college sports would eventually generate for academic institutions, advertising, and media outlets over 100 years later. While the fantasy that student athletes should play solely for the love of the game and amateur sport was the primary argument of the NCAA, the underlying concern was that the competition for the best athletes would be difficult to tame if players could be lured by better financial aid in the form of athletic scholarships offered by their opponents in the conference and nationwide.

It took MSC six tries and John A. Hannah 11 years to gain entry into the conference. Hannah persisted and bent over backward to make the institution compliant with the guidelines for recruiting and eligibility, and he discontinued the Jenison Awards program. While he fundamentally understood that pursuing higher education created a financial hardship for *all* students, and even greater stress on football players, he relented, knowing that being a member of the conference would yield a better football schedule and greater visibility for the institution.

During the time that Hannah struggled for acceptance into the Big Ten Conference, the football roster at MSC consistently included a few Black players from the time of Gideon Smith until after World War II. Although the presence of Black players existed without much fanfare, Horace Smith, a Black All-American running back and track star, caused a bit of a stir in 1946. He was a starter at MSC the full season except for games against Mississippi State and the University of Kentucky. Horace was an incredible athlete and a contributor in terms of running the ball and scoring. While MSC was willing to put its best players on the field regardless of race, the college observed a *gentleman's agreement* when playing schools in the South. Northern schools would effectively bench Black players as a kind of neighborly way of upholding the white supremacy fancied by the *southern way of life.*

By the time Kentucky came up on the schedule in October of the following year, Hannah received a lot of pushback from the Detroit branch of the NAACP after Horace Smith was benched at the Mississippi game. A letter-writing campaign to John A. Hannah, Michigan governor Harry Kelly, and anyone who would listen inspired action. Hannah was responsive and announced to the new head football coach, Clarence "Biggie" Munn, that Horace should play in the game against Kentucky. This refusal to uphold segregation meant that, for the first time, Kentucky would play against a team with a Black player.

The Kentucky team initially refused to come onto the field because of the presence of Horace Smith but ultimately relented, and the result was a close game that MSC lost 6–7. This defiance sent a message to Kentucky and the almost 27,000 people in attendance that MSC wasn't going to back down when it came to starting Black players. By the late 1940s, the institution also boasted a small African American student population, with Black sororities and fraternities on campus who understood the significance of seeing Black players on the field. It was definitely commendable of Hannah to take a stand at a time when it wasn't popular, but for 12 years after this important milestone, MSC avoided southern schools altogether, until 1959.

There's a tiny detail that sealed my father's destiny and eventually that of college athletics as a whole that coincided with MSC's willingness to play southern schools again. John A. Hannah, the president of MSC, was appointed by president Dwight D. Eisenhower to the role of chairperson of the U.S. Commission on Civil Rights from 1958 to 1969. The Commission on Civil Rights was created by the federal government as part of the Civil Rights Act of 1957, which sought to provide a continual appraisal of the status of civil rights in the United States, mainly investigating, documenting, and making recommendations. Among a variety of concerns, Hannah and the members of the commission were tasked with investigating the conditions for Black people living in the American South and other parts of the country.

Essentially, the Commission on Civil Rights and the president of what became Michigan State University were collecting data and reporting on the conditions of Jim Crow just as my dad and Bubba Smith were emerging from its soil. In his tenure as chairperson, Hannah played a key role in the hearings that led to major legislation and court cases, including the Civil Rights Act of 1960, the Civil Rights Act of 1964, the Voting Rights Act of 1965, and the Fair Housing Act of 1968.

As lore has it, during his time with the commission, John A. Hannah made the institution more inclusive. He took action when Black students said they weren't able to get haircuts on campus. In one instance in the mid-1950s, Hannah escorted a Black student to the campus barber to ensure that the student's hair would be cut. He integrated the dormitories and partnered with the Nigerian government to create a university in Nsukka modeled after MSC, which later became an integral foundation of the modern-day MSU African Studies Center. These early initiatives set a tone at Michigan State that made it possible to recruit Black football players on scholarship at a time when my parents couldn't even drink from the same water fountain as a white person or walk in the front door of a white-owned business in their hometowns.

In the 50 years between Gideon Smith's first football game in 1913 and the end of my dad's senior year at George Washington Carver High School in Baytown, Texas, MSC had laid the foundation for the events that would ultimately change my father's life and the trajectory of racial inclusion in college football nationwide.

CHAPTER

FIVE

M y dad was learning his times tables in a one-room schoolhouse for Colored children when Duffy Daugherty was promoted to head coach under athletic director Biggie Munn. Duffy took on the role of head coach in 1954, the same year that the Supreme Court upheld *Brown v. Board of Education*, which ruled that racial segregation in public schools was unconstitutional. Michigan State was an integrated environment, but nationwide, states upholding segregation took their time integrating, including my dad's hometown, La Porte, Texas.

As the new head coach, Duffy had a few lackluster seasons but made significant strides in recruitment, casting his net wider with each new freshman class. With the support of John A. Hannah and Biggie Munn, Duffy's relationships in Hawaii opened the door for talent from the Pacific Islands like William Kaae, who lettered at MSC in 1955. The Hawaii pipeline continued with Larry Cundiff in 1957, followed by Roger Lopes, Dick Kenney, Bob Apisa, and Charlie Wedemeyer throughout the 1960s. The fact that southern schools on the mainland were still dragging their feet on integrating presented Duffy with a unique opportunity to investigate a previously untapped talent pool of Black players in Jim Crow's backyard.

It helped that under Biggie Munn, the team had eight Black players and won the Rose Bowl in 1953. Every team in the Big Ten Conference had at least one Black player, so the climate was right for Duffy to actively recruit Black players from the South at a pace faster than other northern schools. It was simply a matter of determination, will, and infrastructure that made it possible to take full advantage of the plank in the Southeastern Conference's eye at the time. Duffy was an esteemed political figure in the community with just enough social power to be dangerous.

One of his major power moves was the founding of the Coach of the Year Clinics, now sponsored by Nike, with University of Oklahoma coach Bud Wilkinson. The clinics traveled nationwide to provide training and development tools and networking opportunities for high school coaches. When the clinics traveled to the South, the Black coaches couldn't attend workshops with the white coaches, so Duffy's coaching staff, including defensive coaches Henry "Hank" Bullough and Vince Carillot, would lecture in separate rooms and sometimes in alternate venues to accommodate Black coaches.

This approach allowed Duffy and his staff to develop relationships with Black coaches who could help them scout new recruits. They eventually started bringing some of the Black coaches they met to the MSC campus to offer tips for developing players at their all-Black schools in the South. And the Black coaches, having visited the campus, reported back to the Black players and their families about how great the campus was, giving prospects a sense of confidence about what life might be like for them in the North.

Among the high school coaches that Duffy Daugherty courted was a Beaumont, Texas, football coach, Willie Ray Smith, the father of Charles Aaron "Bubba" Smith and Bubba's two brothers, Willie Ray Smith Jr. and Tody Smith. Coach Smith and his wife, Georgia, were known throughout the Golden Triangle region of Texas (Orange, Beaumont, Port Arthur). They were both educated at Prairie View

College, now Prairie View A&M, a historically Black institution. In contrast to the Smiths, my father's parents didn't have the opportunity to go to college because formal education was still an elusive opportunity for many Black Americans in the South at the time. Bubba's parents' college educations granted them access to employment opportunities as teachers in local schools.

Bubba's father fell into coaching in 1942 when the football and basketball coach at the all-Black Dunbar High School in Lufkin, Texas, was sent off to World War II. Coach Willie Ray Smith Sr. didn't know a tackle from a halfback, but he needed a job. Most of the adult men in the area had been called to military service at the time. Coach Smith was shot in the leg trying to break up a heated argument between two brothers in Denton, Texas, back in 1934, so he couldn't pass the physical requirements for military service. His charm and the previous Dunbar High School coach's plays floated him for a few weeks while he learned everything he could about football from a veteran coach in Wichita Falls. The opportunity was serendipitous for him and his wife, Georgia, because she was pregnant with a baby girl, their first child. The Dunbar High School gig offered economic security at a time when they needed it most.

Coach Smith was on the road with his Dunbar football team when Georgia gave birth on October 7, 1942, at her mother's home in Nacogdoches, Texas. They named their new daughter Oreatha Ray, but she died three days after she was born, in part because the local hospital prohibited them and their Black doctor because of segregation. Their doctor was helpless in saving the child once she started showing signs of distress. Like many other Black families who'd experienced similar heartbreak, they pushed through the incredible loss. Coach Smith led the Dunbar team to four district championships by the time the war ended and the original Dunbar coach returned to reclaim his job.

The Smith family grew in size with the blessing of three successful live births, Willie Ray Smith Jr., Charles Aaron "Bubba" Smith,

and Lawrence Edward "Tody" Smith—who would all go on to become
Black pioneers in the game. After a stint in Orange, the family settled
in Beaumont, Texas, when Coach Smith took a position at Charlton-
Pollard High School. After his winning seasons, Coach Smith became
a well-known fixture in the Golden Triangle. To this day, the region
consistently cranks out some of America's best football players and is
now known as the Football Capital of the World.

Coach Smith met Duffy Daugherty at one of Duffy's high school
coaching clinics in Dallas. The meeting led to MSC offering Bubba's
older brother, Willie Ray Jr., a scholarship opportunity. Willie Ray Jr.
turned it down and accepted a scholarship at Iowa. Even though Duffy
wasn't able to win over the first son, he continued to develop a relationship with Coach Smith in hopes that he could help him recruit other
Black players in the region and possibly his son Bubba in 1963. The
entire family would prove to be an important resource as Duffy pursued
prospects in the region. Coach Smith was a father figure to a lot of
young men in the Colored section of Beaumont, and his wife, Georgia,
welcomed his players at her dinner table after she finished a long day
teaching at the local junior high. Duffy's proximity to the Smith family
paid off for a skinny Black boy named Eugene Washington, who played
football, basketball, and baseball, ran track, and happened to live over
an hour away in La Porte, Texas.

My dad is the oldest of the three children born to Henry and
Alberta Washington. They lived as a blended family in the Colored
section of town. My grandmother had a daughter, Mary Lee, and my
grandfather a son, John, and a daughter, Willie Mae, from previous
relationships. Together they had my dad, Eugene, and his younger sisters, Ephenetta and Essie Mae. The Washingtons were a fairly close-knit
family and well liked in the community. They were active members of
Zion Hill Baptist Church and kept the kids on a rather short leash. My
grandfather was a deacon in the church, and my grandmother sang in

the choir. They attended services before and after the regular morning services, followed by afternoon and evening services on Sunday.

On weekdays my dad was bused to George Washington Carver High School in Baytown, Texas, because La Porte Independent School District didn't provide a high school for Black students. Even though La Porte High School was walking distance from home, he was forced to commute about 40 minutes by bus every morning to Baytown, Texas, because of the color of his skin. He was a good student and an incredible athlete. The coaches saw my dad's natural gifts and persuaded my grandfather to allow him to participate in sports. Unlike Bubba's dad, my grandfather had little time for or interest in sports. He was focused on his work and church responsibilities. My grandfather agreed to let my dad participate on the condition that the coaches—Johnny Peoples (football), Robert Strayhan (track), and Richard Lewis (baseball)—give him rides the long distance back to La Porte at the end of the day, since the school buses weren't in service by the time practices let out. The terms of the deal also included transportation to and from games and meets. My dad's abilities eventually caught the attention of a local baseball team composed mostly of adult men in the Black community.

Among the many meaningful treasures about my dad's life that I discovered while working on the documentary film project was the revelation that his first job was at the Port Theatre, a movie house, on Main Street in La Porte. He was responsible for organizing the film reels, changing the marquee, and janitorial tasks. I was grateful to find a point of connection between us. The flickers of light inside a dark cinema house were as familiar to him as theatre auditoriums were to me as a teenager.

In Minnesota, beyond the footlights of the stage, I'd see the hazy, amused faces of white patrons in the audience, which made it easy for me to make out my Black family in the crowd. When my dad worked the cinema projection room in La Porte, Texas, Black patrons, his family and friends, had to enter from a side door and sit in the balcony to view

the films. His employer, Mr. Rigby, followed my dad's athletics and
chatted with him as he attended to his responsibilities of cleaning and
maintaining the Port Theatre between school sports activities. Beyond
Mr. Rigby, my dad had little contact with white people in La Porte. His
world from morning to night was a Black one. The only interaction he
and his family had with white people was through employment. This
extended to his athletic endeavors as well.

Under Jim Crow, the Black community was the lifeblood that kept
families afloat in those days. My dad was surrounded by elders who
looked out for everyone's kids, and not just their own. Whether it was
people at the church, teachers at the school, or neighbors on the same
block, he had the support of "the village," rooting him on as he made
a name for himself at George Washington Carver High School. A lot
of Black folks who grew up in that climate describe it as a bubble. Life
outside of the Black part of town was degrading and suffocating, but
within the community, a self-reliance existed that inspired creativity
and determination to shape better lives, not only for oneself, but for
the greater community and possibly *the race* as well.

Among the infrastructure that the community nurtured was athletic competition with other Black—or in those days, *Colored*—schools.
Carver High competed against other Black schools in the region, among
them Charlton-Pollard High School in Beaumont, Texas, home of
Coach Willie Ray Smith Sr. and his talented children. Their encounters on the football fields, running tracks, and basketball courts within
those all-Black athletic leagues throughout my dad's high school career
led to a conversation that changed my dad's life.

Coach Smith had become Duffy Daugherty's eyes in the area. By
his senior year of high school, Bubba was six foot seven and 300 pounds.
Coach Smith's middle child was being recruited by Michigan State and
other schools around the country that would take Black players. It's
hard to pinpoint the time line in terms of when and how the Smiths
told Duffy Daugherty about my dad. It's likely the camaraderie began

when Willie Ray Smith Sr. coached Bubba and my dad in a high school East-West All-Star Game in their junior or senior year. They developed a friendship, and when my dad heard that Bubba was planning to accept an offer at Michigan State, Coach Smith said he'd put in a "good word" to Duffy Daugherty in hopes they'd consider my dad as well. And he did.

I may not have known a lot about football while growing up, but I was aware that families pay thousands of dollars from Pop Warner youth leagues to high school participation fees in hopes their sons will make it to a Division I school. It seems unlikely that parents in the 21st century would help players from opposing high schools over an hour away get scholarships to their sons' dream schools. Coach Smith cared deeply about the young men in his charge, and he also knew the value of a good education. He understood that his own children, and the Black players in the Golden Triangle, would have to leave segregation if they were to have a shot at a life that was bigger than the one Jim Crow could give them.

Lord, I keep so busy serving my master

Keep so busy serving my master

Keep so busy serving my master

Ain't got time to die

'Cause when I'm giving my all

I'm serving my master . . .

Ain't got time to die

———

Traditional Negro spiritual,

arranged by Hall Johnson in 1956

CHAPTER
SIX

The media cart was the deus ex machina that made middle school bearable, yet nothing could have prepared me for the week we watched *Roots* on VHS in American history class. The images of Black people chained in the dark and musty bowels of a slave ship rearranged the molecules in my brain irrevocably. It was the first time I'd seen the miniseries even though it had been well over a decade since its 1977 premiere. This wasn't the LeVar Burton I knew as the happy Black man who read picture books on TV's *Reading Rainbow*, but a character, Kunta Kinte, whose name was whipped from his body until the lash christened him *Toby*, interchangeable with the proper noun *Nigger*. The Black women characters were repeatedly violated by white men, and a few appeared with bare breasts. The horror I felt in my body was further stirred by chortles from the boys in the classroom. The impossible experience of being the only Black person in the room and one of few in the entire school marked the first time I felt, or was made to feel, shame about my heritage.

The teacher dimmed the lights in the classroom so we could see the screen, but frame by frame, every microaggression that I'd previously passed off as the weirdness and idiosyncratic phenomena of suburban white kids and their families was illuminated. I became aware of how white America saw me and Black people in general. She insisted that the students call her "Ma" instead of Mrs. or Ms. Even though her preferred title positioned her as our middle school matriarch, it felt extremely paternalistic to imagine the old white lady as my mother. It felt as unnatural to me as I imagined it must have been for enslaved Africans to be forced to call a stranger *Master* after being stolen from their villages.

While it was quite commendable that our teacher exposed a group of middle- and upper-middle-class teens to America's twisted relationship with race, she had no clue what her approach to addressing race relations was doing to me or my white classmates. She used terms like *Afro-American,* which drove me nuts because, as far as I knew, there was no country nor continent nor nation called *Afro.* I didn't know the etymology of the word or the journey my ancestors trod from being called a *nigger* to an *Afro-American*, but the word *Afro* set off an uproar of laughter from the white boys, whose voices may have changed over the summer, but their maturity took a nosedive by the start of the school year.

It was a lot to deal with on top of the universal American adolescent struggle. Almost overnight, those same boys who once played baseball with me at the park in front of our house started calling me *Fro* and would routinely spit on the back of my head when they sat behind me in class or on the bus. The blond boy who gave me a ring and had asked me to "go with him" in fourth grade stopped talking to me altogether. I had relentless pimples on my forehead, so the boys started calling the zits on my face *Maya's mountains* when they weren't spitting on my head or calling me *Fro*. Hip-hop had become mainstream by then, and the word *wigger* (*white* + *nigger*) was on the tongue of suburban white kids throughout the land. I hated them for their ignorance and the ways that racism seemed to creep into every square inch of the classroom and the bus rides home at the end of the day.

A racialized pseudo spring awakening hastened the chasm growing between me and my white peers and even my teachers. When the teacher added Scarlett O'Hara, the silly crinolines, and the poor, ignorant Black slave Prissy, who *knew nothing about birthing babies* in *Gone with the Wind*, to the curriculum to point out the overt racism in the depiction of *Afro-Americans* in the famous film, it made me even more frustrated. My thirteen-year-old body boiled with anger, silently refusing to allow her or anyone else to put me in my *place*. Even though my resistance was passive and wholly confined to my adolescent mind, she picked up on my resentments and grew mean toward me. She called me a *jerk* once, but I don't remember what I'd done to provoke such strong midwestern language.

My parents instilled pride in me for being *young, gifted,* and *Black,* but they also taught me to respect authority figures. I believed that there was nothing I could actually *do* about the teacher or the behavior of my classmates, so I found solace in the competition squad at my neighborhood dance studio. I loved dance rehearsals, performance, and the excitement of competitions throughout Minnesota and sometimes on the road in the summer for Nationals. I needed the outlet for self-expression, but racial isolation persisted in that space as well. After weeks of auditions, I made the squad. It was probably a thrilling combination of rBST hormones in the milk we bought from the grocery store and African DNA that made my lean but curvy adolescent physique stand out among the flat-chested, narrow-hipped white dancers in the group. I can remember only a couple other biracial Black girls who were siblings and a few Korean American and mixed-race Pacific Islander Americans in the entire competition program, from five- to six-year-olds to high school seniors.

I was using chemical relaxer on my hair every six months, so I had to roller set my hair into a round, curly halo like the white girls' on the squad. The style was like the bouncy ringlets that Irish dancers from *Riverdance* wore, only teased within an inch of every strand's life.

We'd jazz strut across the stage in our sequins and layers of petticoats over bicycle shorts, in bedazzled shoes, rocking little sponge-curler-set white-girl Afros, blue eye shadow, and red lipstick. For ballet and lyrical numbers, we'd salvage our curls in a hair-netted bun that resembled the single Afro-puff ponytail styles Black women wear today. I was in high school before I realized my natural hair grew out of my head in wavy ringlets. I spent hours rolling my hair for no reason in those days. The biracial Black girls were either much smarter than me, or their white moms couldn't figure out how to roller set their hair, because they happily showed up on competition days rocking their thick, natural, kinky spirals fuss-free.

Dance gave me confidence and much-needed friendships outside of my school environment. I didn't worry *too* much about how different my body was from my dance mates, but the culture of squads in those days, similar to professional ballet today, was precision and uniformity. The flesh-colored tights we were expected to wear never matched my brown skin, and the makeup palettes that were designed for us were usually all wrong for my complexion. I was promoted to the next age level the following year and was relieved to be among older girls who were even curvier than I was. We were often first or second in the state depending on the competition and stood out for our costumes and choreography when we faced smaller dance schools throughout the region.

Since I'd successfully chosen a sport that was *Gene Washington proof,* much of the details of my dance life were on my mom's shoulders. She wrote the checks when they were due, sewed sequined bits and pieces to my costumes, and spent hours roller setting my hair until I was skilled enough to do it myself. Our interactions around my dance training and the minutiae that came with it were often a source of tension. On the one hand, she was my biggest supporter; on the other hand, my dancing was a handy reference point for the litany of parental complaints and threats: *I just paid all this money for your class; you can put the rhinestones on your shoes your damn self!* Or worse, *I'm going to take you out of dance if you don't* (fill in whatever expectation).

As a result, the future of my dance training always felt like it was hanging in the balance. I did whatever I could to avoid the execution of those threats and made sure to get more As than Bs (and never Cs) in school, manage housework, and all that goes with being a good kid. Dance was a lifeline for me, and my mom knew how to leverage it whenever she felt it necessary. Maybe it was working in corporate America or frustration in her marriage, or a combination of all the midlife stressors known, or yet unknown, that women of the boomer generation stuffed in their Playtex 18 Hour bras just to keep up with their work inside and outside of the home. Whatever it was, it was exhausting.

To this day, I'm not sure if my mother resented *me,* the dance studio culture, or the fact that the "dance mom" tasks fell on her and not my dad. I liked that my dad wasn't hovering over me the way he'd coached my sister Lisa in track, so he wasn't particularly present in the day-to-day of my passion, outside of dropping me off or picking me up from class when my mom or friends' parents couldn't. My mom indulged my dance training because she saw it as a way for me to stay out of trouble. I was cool with my dad being checked out of my dance world, because I intentionally wanted it that way. Still, I wished my mom had been more like the other mothers who wore ridiculous buttons and rhinestone-studded, airbrushed jean jackets at competitions in support of their kids.

My mother was in the early years of a born-again Christian journey. The Catholic edition. She became active in a Catholic Charismatic Renewal community, who, like their Pentecostal brethren and sistren, would catch the Holy Ghost and pass out, speak in tongues, or both. Aside from Sunday Mass, my mom attended Daily Mass every morning at 6:30 a.m., observed Holy Days of Obligation, did a 24-hour adoration of the Eucharist on rotation with others at the church, and dutifully maintained the parish prayer chain. She fasted on bread and water three days a week, and every day at 3:00 p.m. central time, she stopped whatever she was doing, whether it was a business meeting or a grocery store run, and prayed the Chaplet of Divine Mercy to mark the hour of Jesus's death.

I observed my mother's religious devotions with both fascination and trepidation. Every few weeks the Charismatic Catholics throughout the Twin Cities would gather for Healing Mass. The venue changed every time, but the format was always the same. A highly theatrical ritual unfolded as people brought their ailments and burdens to the altar. My mother and others who'd received the Holy Spirit would literally *lay hands* on their foreheads and shoulders. I watched from the pew as some would slump over after a few seconds, simultaneously caught in the arms of others who stood at the ready to guide them to the floor. I don't recall anyone leaping out of their wheelchairs or doing a ring shout—it was a Catholic church, after all. But there was a magic and mystery in the air that the congregants committed to with their whole beings. At one point in the service, those with the gift of tongues would surrender a symphony of what by itself sounded like gibberish, but in unison was like a chorus of snake rattles, a rhythmic bell choir, and the vibratory hum of the most pious monks roaring from the catacombs of ancient wisdom, all at the same time.

It was beautiful and also frightening as hell. Sometimes it felt like I'd lost my mother's voice among the hiss of the other tongue speakers. It was almost like watching her devotion to me and our family be swallowed by Mary, God, and the suffering of Jesus. And there was nothing any of us could do about it. I made a pact with God that *I never want the gift of tongues or the ability to understand them*, because I didn't want to lose myself the way it seemed I'd lost my mom to religion. If I'd had a rough day at school or anxiety about being ready for line placement auditions at dance, she'd sometimes stop me midsentence and place her hands on my head and let the thunderous tongues roar. But it rarely actually made me feel better or more confident about whatever was on my mind or heart. I believed that what I was witnessing in the rituals was real, but it wasn't the way I wanted or needed a sense of divine love from my mother in those moments.

Taking my teenage cross to the feet of my earthly father, Gene Washington, wasn't exactly a viable alternative. How and where could I begin to talk about the innermost pangs of my teenage girl heart with my 40-something-year-old dad?

If he caught me moping or releasing an angst-ridden premenstrual sigh followed by "Ughhhh, I'm so tired," he'd look up from his giant bowl of shredded wheat with a grimace and say, "Tired? You're too young to be tired. You have no idea what it's like to be tired."

The dynamic in our household was similar to a lot of emotionally dysfunctional homes in America. Playing the dozens, *yo mama* jokes, and laughing about being hit with shoes, boards, and switches were ways that Black teens commiserated about Black parenting in those days. On the other side of our childhoods, though, most of us have come to the realization that being called *little heifers* (or worse) and *being knocked into next week* aren't anything to laugh at. Unlike my sisters, who attempted to go toe to toe with my parents throughout their teen years, resisting what was overprotective parenting at best and an oligarchy at worst, I retreated into myself until my sisters left for college. The door slamming, yelling, and screaming were exhausting and even scary. I marveled at the way World War III could break out in the kitchen and then magically resolve itself just as company rang our doorbell for Thanksgiving dinner. *Et voilà!* We were the perfectly coiffed and smiling family in the portrait hanging in the dining room.

While my dad and my sisters could volley a pretty intense yelling match between themselves, he didn't yell at me often or even say much to me at all. My mother possessed a low-grade, seething rage right below the surface that became more pronounced in my teen years, even with the Holy Spirit moving through and all around her. She'd bring God, the baby Jesus, the Blessed Mother, and the guilt of a thousand Catholic grandmothers into a tongue lashing if she had to. My voice would crack in defense of myself, holding it as close to together as possible until I'd burst into tears. At times it seemed like nothing I did was good enough—or at least sufficient in avoiding a negative reaction.

When my sisters left for college, the house was usually quiet—except when it wasn't. I figured out how to fly under the radar by keeping the house how my parents liked it, excelling in school, not asking for material things, and doing my best to keep a small footprint. The reward? Dance lessons and less yelling. We always had food in the fridge, clothing on our backs, running water, electricity, and heat in the winter, but sometimes I longed for affirmation.

My parents looked at me like I had three heads when I asked them if they'd compliment me sometimes instead of yelling at me. My dad made a few clumsy attempts.

"The kitchen looks nice," he'd say.

"Thanks," I'd reply.

"Is that a new shirt?"

"No, I've had it for about a year now." I'd shrug.

"It looks nice."

"Thanks."

My parents showed love by working hard to provide a good life for us. Unfortunately their parenting style made it hard for me to learn how to love myself. My self-esteem was like the finely shredded canned Parmesan we kept in the cupboard. Between being the only Black girl in pretty much every setting and pleasing my parents in every scenario, I never had the mental or emotional space to let my guard down. My naturally bubbly personality carried a sad and lonely shadow for years. I think I cried nearly every day between ages 11 and 18. I longed to fit in at school, at dance, and in my family. With my sisters away at college, outside of weekly or daily Mass and Holy Days of Obligation, our interactions were limited to mostly silent car rides with my dad if I was lucky, or a lecture from my mom if I wasn't on the curb with my jacket on like she *told me to be* when she picked me up. I desperately wanted my parents' love and approval, yet consciously invented new ways to avoid them as an act of teenage self-preservation.

The stakes were so high in those first 30 years after civil rights legislation that even as a teenager I understood that my parents would never be what I'd most needed them to be on an emotional level. My parents were *race* people, and also champions of anyone who found themselves at the margins of society. That was the gig. Being Gene and Claudith Washington's children meant that we had to share them with the Black community, the church, and the entire human race. Throughout their careers, my parents were human resources executives at major corporations where people of color and women were gravely underrepresented. Outside of work, they contributed to numerous committees, served as lectors and taught religion classes at church, and had a presence at the annual Martin Luther King Jr. breakfast and other Black community events in the Twin Cities.

If my mother saw anyone with melanin of any kind at the local grocery store, she'd introduce herself, and days later they'd be at our dinner table. I've literally lost count of all the people who have credited my parents as being key to getting their first internship or job, meeting their spouse, or just being a stop on their way to their best life. My mom was even able to help international employees secure and maintain work visas to stay in the United States. Even if we needed more of them at home, their quiet efforts in corporate America and the greater Black community had an impact that can't ever be fully measured.

Their greatest tool in a noble fight against oppression was my dad's insistence that *You have to be twice as good at everything. You have to run faster, you have to work harder, and be the best at everything just to be seen as equal.* They lived this mantra in every fiber of their beings. When I was a teenager and even a young adult, my parents' perfectionism as a form of survival had both a pragmatic and toxic impact on my ability to navigate race and life in general. What on earth can you do if you're born into a culture that has already burdened you with a lifelong responsibility to prove that your life has value?

What today's thought leaders and Black activists have critiqued as *respectability politics* was a form of survival for my parents' generation. They were the first generation of Black southerners to experience basic freedoms, gaining the right to vote without the threat of violence for the first time, not as 18-year-olds but as young adults. The first to attend college, live outside of the South in a white neighborhood, and have their children attend predominantly white school districts without the need for a federal escort.

Respectability politics aside, my parents are fundamentally square people—no drinking, no smoking, and no drugs. These were the values they were taught in their Christian households during Jim Crow, but they'd also seen mental illness, addiction, high blood pressure, and cancer wreak havoc on their family trees. They subscribed to the idea that being upstanding citizens to the 100th power was a pragmatic approach to their family's survival. In a lot of ways, it was. My mother was more outwardly anxious in this regard than my dad.

I attempted to navigate being a teenager and Gene and Claudith Washington's daughter as best I could, for God, for the race, for the community, and for my family name. I was a resilient and outgoing kid who had a lot of friends. Nearly all of them were white. My mother's strictness sometimes emerged in the fear that one of the many Sarahs, Nicoles, and Melissas I was friends with might shoplift or misbehave if she left us unattended at the mall—believing that no matter the circumstances, I'd be the one targeted by racist shop owners or police, even if I had been an innocent bystander.

It seemed far-fetched, but I knew the concern was real. It happened to my sister Gina when she was in middle school. She was hanging with friends at the Wayzata Bay Center, the only mall in the area. A police officer detained her, saying that she was an Indian American runaway.

"I'm not from India," she protested. "I'm *BLACK*!"

Her white girlfriend who was with her attempted to help. "Yeah. This is Gina Washington. She didn't run away."

Although our multiethnic heritage on both sides has rendered my siblings and me with skin tones and features that occasionally confuse people, we were raised with a strong Black identity, and happen to have a lot of family friends who *are* immigrants from India and other parts of Asia. My sister was incredulous at the thought that the police officer in Wayzata didn't know the difference between Black Americans and Indian Americans, or perhaps didn't actually care.

The officer detained them further until my mother showed up to claim my sister. The thing that is so painful about this and other experiences growing up in a white community is the idea that you didn't have recourse in the '80s and '90s as Black people. My parents endured the ignorance and incompetence in order to save themselves and their children's lives. No matter the rage burning in my mother upon seeing her child on a curb at a mall, she had to put it on ice just long enough to appease the officer and get my traumatized 80-pound adolescent sister and her friend home in one piece, away from the spectacle of a parking lot full of white people scrutinizing her every move.

Living with this paradox of late 20th-century psychology that says, "Be yourself" yet "Be perfect," *so white people will accept you and not accuse you of something you didn't do*, is among the many internal conflicts I've had to sort out my whole life. Perfectionism made my parents survivors, the epitome of success in our supposed post-racial America. Having lived to see the first Black president of the United States, I still make large sweeping gestures when I pick up an item and return it to its proper place on a store shelf, so the security cameras catch me *not* shoplifting. I always drive the speed limit, even on long open-highway road trips, because I'm terrified of being pulled over. In my experience, my brown skin in America means I can be treated like an object that's out of its place. My parents did the best they could to preserve their

DNA, the precious cargo the slave traders brought to the continent (and the parts of their blood that were in North America long before) that lives inside them and in us, their children.

All these years later, I see the possibility of freedom from the generational anxiety that afflicted my parents, grandparents, and great-grandparents before them. I was born into the most prosperous generation in my family's history in the United States, and thanks to Title IX, came of age at the most propitious time to be a woman. Even though in America, the value of my life and that of fellow Black, brown, and indigenous citizens is still haunted by the first colonial contact, I know a freedom of thought and movement that my ancestors never could have imagined. For better or worse, I am their shouts to heaven, the rage and sorrow they left at their altars, and every rumble of hope in the deepest hollow of their drums.

CHAPTER
SEVEN

The Colored school my dad attended for elementary and middle school in La Porte, Texas, was recently turned into a museum. The committee, made up of Black elders in the community, is slowly adding photographs and memorabilia to its collection. The whitewashed walls are mostly bare, with a few historical photographs and a portrait of my dad. The little white one-room schoolhouse reminds me of Laura Ingalls Wilder's Little House books I read growing up in Minnesota. As a child, I thought anything old or historical was always white, pretty much like what I saw on TV with Michael Landon and a young Melissa Gilbert when *Little House on the Prairie* became a series.

When I had the opportunity to tour La Porte Colored School with my dad in 2018, I felt an excitement that was never possible as a child visiting white Minnesota historical sites. The local Black community, led by a committee of dedicated elders and Mary Gay, the wife of my dad's former coach Deotis Gay, garnered support from the City of La Porte and the local school board in their efforts to acknowledge and commemorate the past. My dad's accomplishments mean a lot to their community.

They've recognized him in so many ways that it's hard to keep track of all the honors. Working on what became a documentary about his journey, *Through the Banks of the Red Cedar*, in the years after Bubba passed away, coincided with more and more people and organizations celebrating their place in history. In 2013, the La Porte Black community hosted a daylong Black History Month celebration and declared it "Gene Washington Day," featuring proclamations from the City of Baytown and La Porte, which included an appearance by Mayor Louis R. Rigby, the son of my dad's former Port Theatre employer. A small but sincere parade through downtown La Porte culminated in a luncheon attended by mostly Black families living in the neighborhood and our relatives still residing in the area. With the distance of 50 years, I could imagine some of the elders in the room as young people.

During our time at the La Porte Colored School, I started to better understand what my dad's accomplishments meant to Ms. Gay and the Black folks still living in the area. Ms. Gay, coach Deotis Gay, and other Black families shaped and molded the young people of La Porte. They were steadfast in faith and in the love they poured into one another under an oppressive framework that still refused to acknowledge Black people's dignity and God-given autonomy over their own lives.

The elders are time capsules—the living embodiment of the children and young adults who survived the worst humiliations, graver than those that my immature middle school classmates could have even conceived of doling out. My dad effectively fled those conditions when he was recruited by Michigan State and later drafted by the Minnesota Vikings. There is a great deal owed to those who remained in the community, whether by choice or providence, or both. The La Porte Independent School District honored my dad and other diverse community members as Distinguished Alumni of La Porte High School at a luncheon in the school's gymnasium. My dad couldn't attend La Porte High School, even though it was blocks away from his home, because he was Black. In his speech, superintendent Lloyd Graham acknowledged that my dad was gracious to accept the honor of Distinguished Alumni, knowing that La Porte High School had been closed to him and other Black students in 1959 because of segregation. To top it off, Superintendent Graham later surprised my dad with a number 84 La Porte High School jersey during halftime at the homecoming game.

I couldn't help but let the tears fall as I watched my dad on the 50-yard line, waving to an integrated La Porte in the crowd, surrounded by Black, brown, and white cheerleaders. It would have been understandable and even warranted for my dad to refuse the gesture or hold on to a sense of outrage 50 years later. Like Ms. Gay, he, too, is a time capsule. He was once a kid who did good by his family name and put the City of La Porte on the map, even if the city had refused to let him use a public toilet or attend the public high school blocks away from his house. The honor of recognition, juxtaposed with the audacity of stitching his name to a La Porte High School football jersey, seems to be what the 21st century holds for historically marginalized communities.

There are so many people of my parents' generation who never see any form of acknowledgment, let alone atonement, for the wrongs of second-class citizenship. They maneuvered a separate and gravely unequal life as best they could. As their children, we have to carve out our own lives in places and spaces that erase those sacrifices altogether, or when acknowledged, minimize government-sanctioned suffering within the confines of a Black History, Latinx Heritage, Native American Heritage, Asian Pacific American Heritage, Women's History, LGBTQIA Pride, and National Disability Employment Awareness Month.

On that day in La Porte, though, I felt myself holding my breath in outrage at what our country has done, yet exhaling in gratitude for my parents and grandparents, who thought enough of me not to give up. In the Colored school with my dad, I felt the passion of the teachers and students who understood the importance of education. I felt gratitude for the ways my dad's first teachers instilled a love of learning that carried him through every door that opened in his academic life, and the ones that opened in mine.

As we exited the Colored school, a community elder, Betty Lewis Moore, recalled the good times they had on the block, growing up on the Northside. She pointed down the road. "Your grandparents used to live right there."

"Right where?" I asked.

"Down the street there. Mr. Henry had a building next to his house, and he turned it into what we called the *Teenage*. And that's where everybody hung out. Everybody went there," Ms. Lewis Moore said with a smile.

"My aunt Ephenetta told me something about that, but I didn't know what she was talking about. She called it a *café*," I said as I leaned up against the front door.

"There was a jukebox in front, and an area where they sold pickles and candy and cookies. And in the back was seating and a dance area. On the front porch was a place for us to sit and hang out. Mr. Washington did that. He did it mostly for his own kids to have something to do. He was always right there so he could see what they were doing."

This was the most exciting thing I'd ever heard about my grandfather. Any story up until that moment on the steps of the Colored school made him sound like a grumpy old man.

"What was my grandfather like?" I asked, thirsty for more of Ms. Lewis Moore's recollections.

"He was quiet."

"A quiet man who has a place for teenagers to dance? That's crazy." I laughed. "Did you ever see *him* dance?"

"Oh no. He didn't. Now Miss Alberta, your grandmother, was more outgoing," she said with a smile.

I couldn't get enough of her living history lesson. I'd felt removed from my grandparents most of my life mainly because my grandfather died before I was born, and I rarely saw my grandmother growing up, since we lived in Minnesota and she still lived in Texas. My dad and I thanked everyone for opening up the space for us and for sharing the stories.

We hopped into the SUV that we'd rented for the trip and proceeded farther down the road to where his family home once stood. My dad grew quiet as I begged him to stop so I could get out of the car and take pictures and video. All that was left of my dad's childhood home was an empty lot with some lonesome but dutifully green Saint Augustine grass set off from the ditch by the road. At the back of the lot, a mangy climbing tree with a short trunk that twisted like a spine caught my eye. I set my iPhone to video mode and proceeded to make a 360-degree turn, aiming it at the empty lot, the neighboring homes, and then my dad sitting in the SUV. I approached the window with my cell phone toward his face and asked, "What's it like to look at where you used to live, Dad?"

"Well, there's nothing there. It brings back memories I would say, but everything's so new. There's a new house going up there, another across the street—so it's an empty feeling, so to speak. The street is now called Martin Luther King Jr. Drive. When we were here it was just Fifth Street. So a lot of changes have taken place. It's all for the better though," he said, looking out the windshield down the road.

~

To think, Michigan State's offensive line coach Cal Stoll stood on that very street, walked over the little driveway, crossed the ditch, and knocked on the door, meeting my dad and his parents, Henry and Alberta Washington, for a recruitment visit in early 1963. They'd never had a white person in their home before. Cal Stoll set the appointment after coach Willie Ray Smith Sr. and his son Bubba Smith from over in Beaumont told Duffy Daugherty at Michigan State to give Eugene Washington a shot.

My grandmother, Alberta, prepared a few refreshments for the meeting. I can imagine her deep mahogany complexion and sturdy build, moving around the kitchen. She had long smooth arms and legs like my father. My grandmother wasn't a big woman, but she wasn't reed thin either. She carried most of her weight through her middle, balanced by bold hips and thin legs that tread many miles cooking and cleaning in white homes. I wonder what she must have thought as she prepared the home for this white coach to visit. Did she even have time to smooth her fine dark hair as she figured out what she'd cook for the man coming to talk about her son, Eugene?

My grandfather worked for the Pfeiffer Electric Company as a handyman in addition to running the little *Teenage*, which Ms. Lewis Moore described as next to the house. I'm intrigued by how, in their own way, my grandparents had the wherewithal to build a small business in their backyard for local teenagers. They even rented out an apartment on the property to earn extra income and keep their kids close to home. Little did they know that this meeting with Cal Stoll would lead their youngest son farther away from home than they could have ever imagined. Coach Willie Ray Smith and his son Bubba said they'd put in a good word, and the knock at the door was the moment their promise shifted the trajectory of my dad's life.

My aunt Essie remembered not knowing what to think. "We didn't have white men coming to our house, or *anybody's* house on the Northside," she told me as I gathered interviews for the documentary.

They opened the front door to Coach Stoll, a white man from the North, and offered him refreshments. He provided them with a well-rehearsed presentation. He talked about Big Ten football and how great it was at Michigan State and the esteem of playing for winning coach Duffy Daugherty. He yucked it up about the major rivalries with Michigan, Ohio State, and Notre Dame, as my dad, his parents, and my tween-aged aunts sat with reserved expressions. They did their best to follow every word he said.

Once Coach Stoll appeared to be done with his monologue, my grandfather asked the question that seemed to be on everyone's mind: "How will he get to Michigan?"

"He'll take a plane, Mr. Washington."

"A plane?" responded my grandmother, who'd never left the state of Texas since arriving from Louisiana as a girl.

"Yes, ma'am, a plane," Coach Stoll repeated.

"Is all of this *free*?" my grandfather pressed.

"Yes, Eugene will be on a scholarship. He'll play football and his tuition, room, and board will be covered by the scholarship."

It was settled. MSU sent my dad a plane ticket to East Lansing and he was on his way. What he didn't realize was that Duffy had run out of football scholarships, so the university took him on a track scholarship instead. This meant that he'd be required to run indoor and outdoor track *and* play football for Michigan State.

His recruitment trip was a glimpse into what an integrated future could hold. When he boarded the plane, he had no idea what awaited him. Feeling the plane lift off the ground and into the clouds for the first time, my dad took in the awe and wonder of the giant state of Texas growing smaller and smaller, as if he and his fellow passengers had defied gravity.

Throughout the winter and spring of 1963, other Black recruits from the South had similar recruitment visits that resulted in trips from Baton Rouge, Louisiana; Beaufort, North Carolina; Orangeburg and Anderson, South Carolina; Roanoke, Virginia; and South Bend, Indiana. Slowly but surely, Duffy's Black recruitment pipeline became a fairly well-oiled machine.

Duffy and his coaching staff homed in on increasing relationships with Black high school coaches in the South, as well as their colleagues coaching under segregated systems. Occasionally, his friends and coaching colleagues, such as Bear Bryant at Alabama, suggested Black players they'd heard about in their communities but couldn't recruit because of the color of their skin. These stories, recounted by my dad's former MSU coaches Hank Bullough and Vince Carillot, and even a few team-mates, are very much part of the mythology that southern coaches were merely victims of their segregated systems and wanted to help their Yankee colleagues by suggesting players they couldn't take. It feels a little too convenient to me when I hear that Bear Bryant recommended a young Black fullback from Roanoke, Charlie "Mad Dog" Thornhill, in a recruitment swap of Joe Namath, who supposedly couldn't meet the academic requirements at MSU.

Sports historian and author Tom Shanahan was able to debunk the myth while researching his book *Raye of Light*. He found that Bear Bryant and Charlie Thornhill crossed paths at a Roanoke Touchdown Club banquet, but Thornhill had already committed to MSU by that time. It's likely that a white sportswriter who was aware that Michigan State was open to Black players was responsible for telling Vince Carillot about Charlie Thornhill.

Like many of Duffy's Black recruits, when my dad changed planes in Chicago, the integrated world and the logistics of a major airport greeted him. There weren't signs for which bathroom was designated *Colored* or *white*. I can only imagine what it was like to see people moving freely without incident or implication because of the color of their skin for the first time in his life. When he finally made it to East Lansing, one of the coaches picked him up from the airport. Everything was new—the physical terrain, the climate, the friendly white peo-ple greeting him, extending their handshakes and selling Michigan State University in every conversation. When he arrived at the Kellogg Center, the campus hotel, he was taken aback by the opportunity to enter through the front door.

"I'd never stayed in a hotel before. Everything was really different. I mean, I'd never gone *anywhere* in my life, really. And next thing you know? I'm in East Lansing," he recalled as my crew and I captured an interview back in 2014.

"What did you think of it?" I blurted, trying to imagine the magnitude of his experience.

"I thought everything was nice. It was really nice. A big campus. I was interested in seeing where we'd have our classes. The opportunity to get an education was really big, you know? I'd never seen anything like that before."

I'm in awe of the maturity and presence of mind he possessed at 18 years old. My mom and her first cousin Benny in Pomona, California, took me on my final visit to the USC campus during the spring of my senior year in high school. They were by my side for every part of the process. I'd attended the University of Minnesota full time my senior year through a special program called Postsecondary Enrollment Option (PSEO). The program allowed me to earn college credits while still in high school, so I was comfortable on a college campus, but I'd never been that far away from home for an extended amount of time in my life. Having my mom and Cousin Benny accompany me on my visit to the USC campus gave us all a lot of peace during a hectic time. Once I got settled into classes, Benny became my California parent, filling in the blanks for family weekends, dorm move-ins, and everything in between. I was miles away from my parents back in Minnesota, but I was never alone because Benny was always a call and a truck ride away. He'd rescue me when I needed a break from the dorms for the weekend or a ride to the airport when it was time to head back to Minnesota. He moved me into my first, second, third, fourth, and fifth apartments in LA and always made sure the pilot light was lit on the stove and heater before heading home to Pomona.

My dad, on the other hand, had to do *everything* by himself. The Michigan State opportunity was beyond anything Henry and Alberta Washington had ever experienced. Together they had about a sixth-grade education. Nothing in their life could prepare them for what was to unfold for their baby boy. My dad and his parents put their faith in God and trust in the white coaches who'd persuaded him to come and visit, then eventually enroll. When he met with the coaches for breakfast, he was overwhelmed by the number of items on the menu. He'd never been in a restaurant, and he'd never seen or ordered off a menu before. He sat politely and observed the coaches and MSU personnel as they interacted with the young white waitress. She turned to my dad and asked, "What will you be having for breakfast?"

Thinking quickly on his feet, he responded, "I'll have what the coaches are having."

And that was that. In one exchange, he demonstrated that he was flexible and adaptable to following the coaches' lead. Everything was completely brand new and a risk for him, as much as it was a risk for MSU to take on so many Black players who'd never lived in an integrated environment.

During the rest of the trip, he took in the facilities and met a few of the current players. To his comfort and delight, a few of them were Black. Sherman Lewis from Louisville, Kentucky, Dewey Lincoln from Hamtramck, Michigan, and other Black players on the MSU team were key to welcoming the Underground Railroad's recruits. Their successes paved the way for Duffy Daugherty to recruit Black players—more than doubling the Black representation with the recruiting class of 1963. The presence of other Black students at MSU was a major selling point. While my dad had only MSU as a major option, other Black recruits— like Bubba Smith, George Webster, Ernie Pasteur, Clinton Jones, and Jim Summers—had the opportunity to visit other major midwestern campuses. Sherman Lewis, who would later go on to become an NFL coach, and other Black players making major contributions helped Duffy seal the deal during the campus visits. It gave a sense of assurance to the recruits that they would be in good company if they made MSU their choice.

Recruiting more Black players than they'd had in any previous incoming freshman class was a gamble for the MSU coaches, but they'd perfected their approach over the years and hoped it would pay off with the addition of other recruited Black players, including Jeff Richardson, Maurice Haynes, James Hoye, Solomon Townsend, and John Whitworth. For the first time, Daugherty and his coaches would have the opportunity to fully execute this experiment and stack the roster with the biggest, fastest, and strongest talent they could recruit from all over the country, including Hawaii, with special attention given to the segregated South.

A lot was at stake on both sides. Michigan State had a football team to backfill with talent, but Lansing, Michigan, still had some room to grow when it came to race relations. Housing was still segregated, and opportunities for Black residents in Michigan's capital were limited in 1963. Although John A. Hannah worked with governor George W. Romney and others at the time to address the overall challenges Michigan faced as part of the state Civil Rights Commission, Duffy Daugherty faced pressure from whites in the community who resented the addition of Black players on scholarship.

Never mind that Ernest Green of the Little Rock Nine had found respite at Michigan State after receiving an anonymous scholarship, which is rumored to have been sponsored by the MSU president, John A. Hannah—there was still a duality to this experiment of Duffy Daugherty's. He had the political currency of a boss who believed in equality and integration, but he'd have to prove that Black talent was key to winning football games. It was a calculated risk and he believed it was worth taking. For my dad and his teammates, most of their scouting was based on their stats from high school. There weren't reels and reels of film displaying their talents or hype videos set to music as you see in recruitment today. My dad was ranked nationally in track, but had limited competition opportunities and received little recognition as a Black athlete in Texas. Michigan State really had no idea of what my dad would eventually bring to the track and football teams.

For my dad and his teammates, the prospect of receiving a scholarship to college was filled with great risk as well. If they didn't make it, or things went awry, they could be sent home and back to Jim Crow. The question of whether they could make it in an integrated environment socially and academically weighed on them, but this opportunity at Michigan State was their best shot at a better life for themselves and their families. Fortunately for Duffy Daugherty, 11 recruits accepted their spots at Michigan State.

For my mother, who my dad describes as his high school sweetheart at George Washington Carver, the idea that Eugene Washington was going to attend college at Michigan State on scholarship was an amazing splash of small-town news. The opportunities for recent Black high school graduates were limited. There were opportunities to pursue trades, work in the local oil refineries, or go to a historically Black college or university to become a teacher, and in some cases, enter a career in science and medicine. College was out of reach for most in their communities because they came from humble backgrounds—and in my mom's case, large Catholic families.

Two of her older sisters followed a Creole migration to San Francisco and started families. My mother's post–high school plan was to live with her sister and attend junior college at Contra Costa. While my parents weren't formally committed to each other, the mutual dedication to furthering their education and achieving their goals and dreams inspired them to keep in touch as they prepared to leave their hometowns.

As my dad and I continued our drive back to Baytown where my mom's family lives, we pulled into the parking lot of Sylvan Beach to have a look at the water. We sat in quiet for a bit, watching the water from the windshield, the way I often take in the Pacific Ocean when I'm in Los Angeles, or at any of the 10,000 lakes in Minnesota. I'd been to Sylvan Beach a few times to visit the La Porte Bay Area Heritage Society on a solo mission for research purposes, and once to fish off the pier with my cousin Mike and my nieces when they were little. It occurred to me in that moment that my dad enjoys the calm and serenity of water against a quiet shoreline as much as I do.

Heading back to the main road, my dad turned right instead of left out of the Sylvan Beach parking lot. As we continued on our way, I began to see a different side of La Porte for the first time in my life. The winding, tree-lined road led us past waterfront properties—some behind gates, others with inviting driveways. It was like stepping into another world that was both completely new yet familiar at the same time. We could have been driving down Highway 101 around Lake Minnetonka near the small town where I grew up, or up the Pacific Coast Highway in Southern California where I came of age.

"Wow, I never knew this was even here. It kind of reminds me of Wayzata, Dad."

"Yeah, these are all summer homes. This is Sandy Point. A lot of vacation homes. How about that?" he said as his eyes moved between the properties and the road.

"I'd love to live in one of those houses. Did you know that's my dream, Dad? I want to live in a waterfront property and host artist retreats someday."

"I did *not* know that. Well, you could get one of these." He smiled, daydreaming with me as we passed the houses.

It felt strange and wonderful to share a daydream with my dad. I am every dream he couldn't possibly have imagined as a boy raised under endless constraints. For me to dare to share my lofty vision of lakefront property in his hometown, and for him to affirm it in the same breath, filled my eyes as I inhaled deeply and directed my focus out the passenger window.

The ghosts of class separation still hovered over the summer homes in a way that reminded me of the land history in the area where I grew up. Lake Minnetonka, *Bde ia taåka* in the Dakota language, literally means "Big Talking Lake." The area was unknown to Europeans for thousands of years before it became a series of resort towns. The US government took possession of the land as part of the Treaty of Traverse des Sioux and the Treaty of Mendota, both in 1851. Within a few years, the majestic lake became the literal talk of the town for commercial developers and white settlers. The treaties resulted in economic devastation, displacement, and starvation for Dakota people throughout Minnesota. Lake Minnetonka has remained a nearly all-white area for close to two centuries.

While I was in the car with my dad, my mind continued to wander, contemplating the ways that Europeans staked claim to the best property, knowing full well it wasn't their right to take it, then gave it to their descendants to do whatever they want with it for hundreds of years—how it didn't matter if I grew up in the North and my dad grew up in the South. The original inhabitants suffered the same fate.

I suspect this awareness of ancestral loss is a familiar experience for African-descended and indigenous North American people—even Japanese Americans who lost their land when they were forced into internment camps during World War II. So much of who we are, and who we were in relation to European contact, survives in direct relationship to our elders. It's a peculiar sort of pain considering how my dad, or *anyone* for that matter, could grow up in such a beautiful place under such suffocating constraints—limited in where they could go and what they could be. Who could dare to dream of something different or better? They were so isolated that before television and national publications, there wasn't a lot of tangible imagery around them to inspire the kinds of dreams I imagine for myself.

If you didn't know the full history of the Black experience in America, this almost island-like place called La Porte, Texas, would feel like a charming little resort town. The steely San Jacinto River runs through Galveston Navigation Channel and eventually to the Gulf of Mexico like something out of a postcard. About a mile down the road, my dad pulled over to the dirt path leading to the

Colored beach where the Black families in La Porte could swim and cool off on a hot and humid afternoon when he was growing up. The path was closed off and surrounded by tall wild grasses. I imagined my dad as a little boy walking with other Black children down the path to the beach and finding a sense of joy in her rocky shore—the twisted logic of racists who needed their own separate *white* beach, somehow ignoring the fact that the same water the Black people swam in passed through their properties and the *whites-only* beach.

It was all the same water, I thought with an exhale. In the distance, the cargo ships and port business muddled on with long rectangular box containers at Morgan's Point, an area that inspired the legend of the "Yellow Rose of Texas," Emily West. Emily was said to have been a free mixed-race Black woman who was indentured to Colonel James Morgan, who claimed the area initially established as New Washington in the mid-1800s. Her fair complexion and beauty were compared to the petals of a yellow rose. During the Mexican-American War, the Mexican troops led by Santa Anna burned the plantation and took Emily captive. She is said to have "entertained" Santa Anna to the point that he fell into a deep sleep after what was more than likely a forced sexual encounter. He was so disarmed that Sam Houston's troops were able to reclaim the area and capture Santa Anna. She is credited for ending the war, but modern anthropologists have uncovered the true inspiration for the "Yellow Rose of Texas" song. It's not actually a war anthem, but fragments from a love note written by a long-lost love, a Black man, who once searched for her when they became separated. The last verse reads:

> Oh, I'm going now to find her
> For my heart is full of woe
> And we'll sing the songs together
> That we sang so long ago

We'll play the banjo gaily
And we'll sing our sorrows o'er
And the yellow Rose of Texas
shall be mine forever more

As my dad and I made our way out of Morgan's Point, the remnants of La Porte's history faded behind us as a reminder that every human city has a story, and so do we.

CHAPTER
EIGHT

On August 28, 1963, nearly 250,000 people gathered in Washington, DC, for the March on Washington for Jobs and Freedom. In East Lansing, the spirit of Martin Luther King Jr.'s dream ushered in the beginning of the school year and my dad's new life as an MSU Spartan. The Black players, especially those who'd left the segregated South, had an instant connection with one another. They didn't discuss the details of what life was like for them under Jim Crow. They had a quiet understanding of what they'd all been up against and the stakes ahead for them as individuals and eventually members of the varsity team. The destiny of Daugherty's career and John A. Hannah's work through the Commission on Civil Rights was inextricably linked to this recruitment effort and its successful implementation.

It helped that my dad's high school opponent with a personality as big as his frame, Charles Aaron "Bubba" Smith, from Beaumont, Texas, was now his teammate. Bubba vied for the alpha male position in every situation. His sense of humor rendered him either a fun-loving prankster or the team bully, depending on what side of the joke you were on. He didn't mess with my dad so much because they had a mutual respect coming from rural Houston, but Bubba threw his size around just enough to get under a few folks' skin.

Also joining the freshman squad was a tall, quiet rover back, George Webster, from Anderson, South Carolina. He quickly acquired the nickname "Mickey" because of his widow's peak hairline, which resembled Disney's famous mouse. George "Mickey" Webster had a commanding presence on and off the field. His smoky voice and coffee complexion made anyone with a pulse forget how to breathe, mesmerized by his great stature and panther-like grace. Mickey was fast friends with another Black recruit, Ernie Pasteur from Beaufort, North Carolina. The two met on a recruitment trip to the University of Minnesota.

My interest in football grew stronger with the help of my dad's former teammates. Ernie Pasteur and his wife, Micki, welcomed me into their home while I was gathering interviews. Ernie's wide smile and laughter reminded me of his "Wonder Boys" story he shared at Bubba's house the night before the memorial. I sat down with him, hoping to glean every last drop of information I could. Ernie gave me the play-by-play of his Minnesota visit, sitting in his Spartan-themed man cave.

Like Duffy Daugherty, University of Minnesota head coach Murray Warmath was among those in the Big Ten who were open to Black players. Minnesota's Carl Eller, Bobby Bell, and Sandy Stephens all made names for themselves in college and professional football. Minnesota had come a long way in race relations since the 1923 Jack Trice tragedy, so the prospect of being a Golden Gopher was viable for Ernie and George "Mickey" Webster.

"Carl Eller took us around. Then Bobby Bell took us around . . . and one bad thing about Minnesota, when we went there it was January. We went to Michigan State in the summer. Beautiful day, sun was out, no snow. Minnesota in January? They had eight inches of snow. I came from North Carolina; Webster came from Anderson, South Carolina. We looked at each other and we didn't hear a word they said about going to school when we looked at that snow!" Ernie said as his eyes widened.

I let out a little knowing laugh. Minnesota winters are truly the worst. No matter how many years I've lived there. I can't handle more

than about a month of Minnesota winter before I start losing my mela-
nated mind.

Ernie continued, "After we returned home, Mickey and I called each
other and talked one another into Michigan State. It was a no-brainer
for me; it was a no-brainer for him."

The relationships my dad had with his teammates and their love for
Michigan State intrigue me more than anything they eventually accomplished on the field. For me, my time at USC had its ups and downs.
The long-term friendships that developed between them at Michigan
State transcend the institution itself. Throughout the filming of the
documentary, I was surprised by how many of them had shrines to
Michigan State in their homes, or how they would show up for their
interviews in head-to-toe Spartan apparel. Until I visited Ernie's man
cave, I thought the whole "sports shrine" room was unique to my dad.

It still weighs on my heart that I never had the opportunity to
thank Bubba Smith before he died for recommending my dad for his
scholarship at Michigan State. Through that gesture, a world that was
previously off-limits because of the color of his skin opened to my
father. His life and the lives of many others were forever changed on
the banks of the Red Cedar River in the 1960s. Every moment I get to
spend with my dad's teammates and their families resolves some of that
regret. With every story they tell, I learn more about their history and
also my own. Among my favorite revelations is that at the last minute,
Duffy managed to add a jovial halfback from Ohio, Clinton Jones, to
the team. He got one of the last scholarships and would play football
and run track, just like my dad. Clinton and my dad became almost
inseparable running track together.

Teammates and coaches called them the Bobbsey Twins. They both
came from devout Christian backgrounds and had high school sweet-
hearts back home (my dad had my mom, and Clinton had a girl named
Toni), so they mostly kept their heads in the books when they weren't at
track or football practice. The two were so inseparable that Duffy would

sometimes call my dad *Clinton*, and call Clinton *Gene*. A brotherhood developed between them that's still solid over 50 years later.

After Bubba passed in 2011, I often spent hours on the phone with Clinton, telling him about the latest fundraising challenges I was facing on the documentary project. Clinton and his family are practicing Buddhists, so it was easy to lean on him as a source of spiritual support and mystical wisdom. I didn't realize that I'd gain an uncle and a father figure in Clinton while I was in the process of getting to know my dad. My dad is good at the stoic pragmatic stuff; Clinton is a bit more on the mushy spiritual side, which is right up my alley. Whenever I see his name on my caller ID, I know I'm in for at least an hour-long conversation. And I enjoy every minute.

The biggest adjustment for my dad was leaving his town of less than 5,000 people and arriving on the East Lansing campus with slightly under 30,000 students. He felt fairly well prepared for his classes by the time he took his seat in the classroom, but getting acclimated in an integrated, predominantly white environment took time. The large class sizes and the nuances of interacting with white students were major adjustments for Black players who'd otherwise had no contact with white people before their time at Michigan State. On move-in day at Wonders Hall, my dad was surprised to find that his roommate was a friendly white guy on the swim team named Gary Dilley. He was taken aback, but he and the future Olympian got along just fine—*swimmingly* even.

I count the fact that he had an accepting roommate as an amazing grace. In the 21st century, one of the biggest challenges students of color face at predominantly white institutions is adapting to the prevailing campus culture. When I filled out my housing applications for USC, I opted to live on Somerville Place, named for the first African American graduates of the dental school. The residential community was on the fifth floor of Fluor Tower, a special interest housing floor dedicated to students interested in learning more about African American culture.

This was coded language for *this is where the Black kids live.* In my application essay for Somerville Place, I expressed how important it was to have a Black community to return to at the end of a day of classes where I might be the only Black student in a lecture hall of 200 or more.

Even though I was in the National Honor Society, started college coursework at the University of Minnesota at age 16, was a Minnesota Governor's Scholar, and had to undergo a competitive audition process for my place in the BFA acting program, I still anticipated antagonism from white students with assertions that I was admitted to USC only because of affirmative action. I'd spent most of my childhood pursuing my academic goals and creative opportunities in the arts, but I always understood that I would be judged by the color of my skin no matter how exemplary my resume. I could use public restrooms and attend public schools, but I always felt a shadow of suspicion from the white gaze questioning how and why I was in a predominantly white space.

I applied to live on the Somerville Place housing floor at USC mainly because I was afraid that I'd travel 3,000 miles away from home and end up with a racist roommate. I'd been to summer camp and dance competitions with lovely but clueless white kids who'd ask harmless yet annoying questions about my hair products or skin care. I'd successfully attended all-white schools my whole life, but at the end of the school day, I returned to affirmations of my Blackness in my parents' home. I saw living on Somerville Place as an insurance policy that if I didn't get along with my roommate on an all-Black dorm floor, at least it wouldn't be because of my race.

It's strange to consider how little my dad claims he thought about race. It wasn't as nuanced for him as it was for me. It was literally *Black* and *white.* He couldn't even use the public bathrooms or drink from a water fountain in his hometown. His presence at Michigan State was historically more significant than mine at USC, and he approached it with extreme grace, focus, and patience. He was grateful for a place to stay, a meal plan, and the opportunity to get an education. At Michigan

State he had a freedom of mobility that he and other Black teammates from the South had never experienced.

From his perspective, all he had to do was excel on the field and the track and keep up with his studies. He was so grateful for the opportunity that any microaggressions he may have encountered rolled off his beautiful brown back when he smoked everyone during drills. I didn't realize that my dad hadn't always been a wide receiver until he explained how he'd earned a starting position moving into his sophomore year. There was a lot of competition, so he had to find his niche. There could only be one number-one starter, so he wanted to be the best in the position. When he was in high school he played end, quarterback, and defensive back. Strategically he thought he'd have a better chance of making it as a wide receiver, because it complemented his speed as a runner. His instincts were right, and he quickly caught the eye of his coaches and his fellow teammates.

As new recruits, the men in Duffy's 1963 class were ineligible to play varsity football. They played on a freshman team and were primarily responsible for preparing the varsity team for their games during scrimmages every week. The varsity team was ranked fourth in the AP Poll by November 1963, with only one loss to USC, and a tie at Michigan. The freshmen made sure the squad was ready for each game. Sometimes they were even reprimanded for going too hard on the practice field. Bubba Smith and George "Mickey" Webster became good friends and would soon prove to be formidable defensive forces. The freshman squad sometimes became so intense that Duffy Daugherty had to stop the practices for fear his varsity team would get hurt before they even set foot on the field on Saturday. The Black players had a lot to prove and worked hard to make sure they stood out, even if it meant getting a little aggressive during practice.

Just as they were starting to get their licks in at Michigan State, president John F. Kennedy was shot in Dallas, Texas, on November 22, 1963. My dad's 19th birthday was the following day. He'd only been in East Lansing a few months since leaving the state of Texas, and the president of the United States, who'd worked with MSU's own John A. Hannah on establishing a more inclusive American society, was *gone*. The varsity game against Illinois was canceled and rescheduled for Thanksgiving Day, November 28, 1963. The Spartans lost the game and came in second in the conference behind Illinois, and ninth in the country in the AP Poll.

My dad found a rhythm in East Lansing, which was growing colder as fall pressed into winter. While he was absorbing all of the incredible opportunities before him, things shifted dramatically for his family back home. After he left for school, my grandmother abruptly announced to my aunts in the middle of the night that she was leaving our grandfather and moving to Houston. I was dumbfounded when I sat across from my aunt Ephenetta, my dad's younger sister, as a casual conversation about what life was like when my dad went off to Michigan State changed everything I thought I knew about my grandparents. I didn't spend a lot of time with my dad's family growing up. My mother's family dominated our time when we'd visit the Houston area, leaving a few hours to spend with my dad's side of the family before we'd leave town. He never mentioned his parents' separation, so I'd never thought to ask.

If my determination to learn everything I could about Bubba's and my dad's journeys hadn't inspired a full-on interview with Aunt Ephenetta, I never would have known that my dad's family was in upheaval while he was at Michigan State. Life was extremely unstable for my grandmother and her daughters during that time. With this detail filled in, I better understand why my dad didn't return home often while he was in college. I always assumed it was because at some point he'd have to move from the front of the bus to the back on the interstate trips home to La Porte and confront the racism that pervaded every aspect of waking life for Black people in the South. I realize now that the idea of home itself might have been hard to navigate as well. I can only imagine what inspired my grandmother to up and leave in the middle of the night. I was both stunned and impressed that she felt she had enough agency as a Black woman in 1963 to leave. Or that it was so bad that she subjected herself to poverty and strife to do it. As if at once, I realized why my dad always makes a point to mention the number of years he and my mother have been married in his public speeches. His marriage is a source of pride and accomplishment to him.

It was a lot to take in for me. My being was filled with grief for my aunts and also for my dad. To this day I've never discussed it with him. What's even harder to swallow is that I barely knew my grandmother. She'd only traveled out of Texas a couple of times that I can remember—a trip to East Lansing when my dad was honored by the inaugural class of the MSU Athletics Hall of Fame and my dad's 50th birthday party in Minneapolis. My grandmother was a quiet woman. As a small kid and as a teenager, I didn't have the maturity to understand how to even make conversation with her. I wish I'd asked her about every inch of her life when she was alive. Oral history is all that many Black and indigenous families have in the United States. Who we were, how we lived, who we loved or had to leave and why aren't always on the US census records. There was some grace in her last year of life when I had the chance to reach out by phone. She had an inoperable brain tumor that caused seizures. I didn't fully understand her medical problems, but I knew it was serious and our time together was limited.

During my calls from my dorm at USC, we mostly talked about the same things we talked about my whole life—the weather and how she was feeling. "I'm doing all right. I just got a little arthritis, but I'm all right," she'd say lightly.

We'd always keep things pedestrian, starting with the weather, followed by how I was getting along in my classes. There's never an ideal or appropriate time to ask our elders the questions we don't even realize—that somewhere inside of us—we are dying to know the answers to. If only I'd had the foresight to ask my grandmother about her childhood, the first time she fell in love, what she thought about segregation, or what her life was like when my dad left home.

My sisters, on the other hand, spent a few weeks every summer in La Porte as kids and later as teenagers. They have wonderful stories about sleeping on the front porch on the hot, humid nights to stay cool. My grandmother apparently had reunited with my grandfather and took care of him toward the end of his life when he lost his leg to diabetes. As I was pulling Super 8 reels my dad had made during the '60s, '70s, and '80s for the documentary, I uncovered a sweet film of my grandparents sitting at the dining room table. It may even be the table my sister had shipped to Minnesota and refinished. Actually, it's probably the same table where the MSU coach sat and persuaded my grandparents to let my dad attend Michigan State.

In the footage, my grandfather is sitting at the table holding his chin in one hand with a soft closed-mouth smile. My grandmother is walking around behind him and smiling at the camera as wide and wonderful as my dad when he's filled with joy. It's hard not to feel like I missed out on this level of interaction and sense of relationship with my grandparents. My grandfather passed before I was born, and my grandmother was an aging woman by the time I came around. I can tell that she was warm and kind through the clips of her holding hands with my siblings as preschoolers, then hugging my mother as they walked around the Como Zoo in Minnesota in the 1970s. My dad's film captured the sweetness of their early family life—a reminder that my parents and siblings perhaps lived an entire lifetime together before I was born.

By the time I was old enough to fly by myself, my siblings were young adults off at college or in graduate school. Usually someone from my mom's family in Baytown would make the drive to drop me off at my grandmother's senior apartment community for a few hours. We'd usually sit and watch soap operas or judge shows. She'd ask me if I was hungry, and I'd shrug or say no. Eventually my grandmother would leave to go visit with a friend down the hall and come back to her unit where I was waiting after a while. I didn't know how to spark anything different between us and neither did she. When I started working in film and television as an actor, I always hoped maybe I'd be cast in a soap opera so she could watch me from her living room. I got a small part as a day player on *The Young and the Restless* once, but it was years after she'd died in her sleep on Valentine's Day.

When she passed away, we all headed to Texas for her funeral. My dad's sisters did most of the heavy lifting when it came to the service and all the details. The floral arrangements and almost everything else were pink, which I found out was her favorite color. At the funeral service, I was a sponge when it came to every fact I could learn about her. She had a nickname, "Ninny," given to her by her sister in childhood when she was scared of the goats on the family farm. I even met my grandmother's sister at the funeral. I hadn't even realized she had a sister. I sat on the pew next to my dad at the service. He had a stoic and peaceful composure throughout. One by one, different family members approached the lectern and shared their memories. I felt grateful to hear delightful stories about my grandmother, and sad that I didn't have a lifetime's worth of memories like everyone else did. I wished I'd had more contact with her in my childhood. I felt regret that I hadn't asked for it, but frustration that my parents hadn't done more to facilitate it. Alberta Washington was the only grandparent I'd actually met, and she was gone.

My cousin Marquita, Aunt Ephenetta's daughter, performed the song "Angel" by Sarah McLachlan to close out the morning. I was in awe of my cousin in that moment. Marquita was always one of those precocious, tomboyish, know-it-all kids with glasses and all kinds of opinions about everything when we were growing up. At our grandmother's funeral I saw the brilliant young woman she'd become. Angelic notes poured off her body like silk and cracked my heart open. I looked over at my dad and saw his shoulders shaking as he covered his face with one hand. I'd never seen him cry before. I haven't seen him cry since.

CHAPTER
NINE

M y parents came of age barely a century after their once-enslaved ancestors were emancipated. After years of strife, legislation, and activism in the form of sit-ins, boycotts, and other nonviolent political action met by assassinations, bombings, and lynchings, president Lyndon B. Johnson signed the Civil Rights Act of 1964 into law. The legislation was the culmination of the work of Michigan State University president John A. Hannah, as chairman of the U.S. Commission on Civil Rights, and about 100 years of grassroots activism and Black resilience. In an effort to chronicle the social and political journey of African Americans since emancipation, under John A. Hannah, the U.S. Commission on Civil Rights published two significant reports based on years of fact-finding and investigation: *Freedom to the Free: Century of Emancipation 1863-1963*, and *Civil Rights '63*. In October 1963, *Civil Rights '63* was delivered to President Kennedy a mere month before he was assassinated on November 22, 1963.

These exhaustive reports placed the harrowing struggle for basic human rights of "Negro citizens" into historical context for the United States government. Although the doctrine of "equal opportunity" had existed in the United States since the Declaration of Independence, the Bill of Rights, and subsequent Constitutional Amendments 13, 14, and 15, by 1963 the commission came to appreciate and acknowledge the extent to which failures in the implementation of that doctrine had impacted Black Americans. The opening paragraphs of the *Civil Rights '63* report shrewdly articulate what my parents, grandparents, and great-grandparents lived.

> Until recently, however, the growing discontent of Negroes did not manifest itself in overt action compelling the Nation's attention. Thus it was possible for other Americans to believe that the activities of civil rights organizations did not reflect any strong dissatisfaction on the part of the Negro community at large. The events of 1963 have shattered this illusion. Negroes throughout the Nation have made it abundantly clear that their century-old patience with second-class citizenship is finally at an end.

Growing up *Colored* in American society meant my parents' generation had to be a people of false obedience. They followed the social and legal protocols of Jim Crow, not because they enjoyed being treated as subhuman, but in service of basic survival. Without federal protections in the form of civil rights legislation, they had no recourse for the treatment they received or the fear that permeated their basic activities, like buying property, groceries, and supplies, or gaining dignified employment to buy said property and supplies. Segregationist policy rooted in deep white supremacist beliefs created a hostile climate for Black people daring to resist racism and even for those, like my parents and grandparents, who were still maintaining "false obedience" as a form of survival.

In my dad's case, the thin veil of economic class and status as a sports figure protected him at Michigan State and later with the Vikings, probably more powerfully than the sad-looking helmets and protective pads he wore on game day. It's an uncomfortable reality, because my father's talent, drive, and unfettered determination are his own. He had the promise and potential of any other young person coming of age at the time, but white supremacy, in practice, put physical restraints in the forms of laws and *customs* on what he could achieve. There were Black men throughout Texas with just as much promise who never saw a fraction of the opportunities that attending Michigan State afforded him.

If I've learned anything about race in America, it is the uncomfortable truth that my safety as a Black person, and as a woman of color, is in direct relationship to whiteness. Among the few stories my mother is willing to talk about from her childhood is the time she was tasked with driving my grandmother and great aunt to a doctor in Highlands, Texas, an all-white area at the time. She was a new driver and wanted to make the trip last a little longer. She thought enticing them with a stop at the malt shop might grant her more time behind the wheel.

"Wouldn't you like to get a malt, Mother? Aunt Rosalie?" she said with lilting joy.

"No! I wouldn't like a malt. I want to go home," my grandmother snapped.

My mom knew they wouldn't actually be able to *go inside* because it was *white only*, but she was still excited that they'd be able to order from the back of the store. My mother proceeded to ignore my grandmother and turned down the small road toward the malt shop. My grandmother wasn't having it.

"If you don't turn this car around, there's going to be trouble," she scolded.

"But, Mother, it's right *there*. We'll just go to the back door real quick," my mom pressed her.

"I said, turn this car around!" my grandmother demanded.

My mom heeded the warning this time, and started to turn into a yard, in order to turn the vehicle in the other direction. As she backed up, the wheels of the car got mired in the lawn. She started to panic and realized she'd turned onto soft ground. As she backed out of the lawn, the wheels kicked up a section of the sod. My mom was scared. My grandmother and great aunt were petrified.

My grandmother, approaching hysterics, yelled, "Look what you have done, little girl! You've torn up these people's yard!"

The white homeowners came running out of the house, and the police showed up on the property moments later. My grandmother tried to defuse the situation, explaining why they were in these white people's yard, and that they didn't mean any harm.

The white policeman started interrogating my mother. "Do you know what trespassing is?"

Before my mother could even begin to form a response, my grandmother started name-dropping the powerful white family that my mom's brother, Burnice Junior, worked for.

"My son works for Patterson's Bakery. He's been working for them awhile. We're very sorry." My grandmother pleaded on repeat: "The Pattersons know my son. He's a baker for them at the bakery. He started working for them after he came back from the Marines."

She used the words "Patterson's Bakery" and "my son" probably a hundred times until my grandfather and great uncle arrived. They sorted things out with the officer, offering to replace the sod. The white family agreed not to press charges, and they were on their way. It's hard to get many stories about my mom's childhood out of her, but this one she's always been fairly open to talking about.

It was a pivotal moment for her. It's one of a few memories where she can clearly articulate the impact that racial discrimination had on her, and maybe the way it informed how she parented her own kids. "I was so scared, because it was like, you know, no major crime had been committed, and I realized in a way that I've never forgotten exactly what my parents meant, about having to be safe. Something happens to the psyche of a child. When you always have to worry about being safe. What I did was foolish, but it wasn't criminal. I was treated like a criminal," she told me over a cup of tea some 50 years later.

My grandmother's only tool for diffusing the situation was mentioning that my uncle worked for Patterson's Bakery. The Pattersons were a wealthy and well-respected white family. "I thought, why in the world was Mother talking about Junior working at the Patterson's Bakery? It was just so weird to me," my mom said, shaking her head. "I knew what she was doing, but our parents were so afraid for us. And Black men especially at the time had no recourse. So, if somebody said you did something, you may get hauled off or harmed by the police. We were just harassed, and that was a fact of life."

It's stunning to me the way that proximity to the Pattersons, who were white, served as a mantle of protection for my grandmother. If America were to flirt with the possibility that all men and even women were, in fact, created equal, in the eyes of the law, it would require the participation of the white establishment. White people had to be convinced that discrimination was unconstitutional even if they didn't find it morally wrong. Through the various studies and publications of 1963, the Kennedy administration grew to understand that legislation was required to enforce the right to vote and protect the constitutional rights of all citizens facing discrimination on the grounds of *race, color, religion,* or *national origin*. Upon signing the legislation, president Lyndon B. Johnson made the possibility of receiving injunctive relief against discrimination in public accommodations more tangible for my parents' generation.

I first learned about the Civil Rights Act of 1964 in high school, but I came to understand the climate surrounding the legislation when, as a teenager, I was cast in a production of *Freedom Riders* at Youth Performance Company in Minneapolis. My character in the play was a Student Nonviolent Coordinating Committee (SNCC) worker from the North traveling to Mississippi for the Freedom Summer of 1964. I had about three lines in the entire play, but the experience changed my life and reshaped my understanding of the place of young people in civil rights history. It was an opportunity to create meaningful art with

Black and white teens from urban areas, and from the suburbs like me. We watched hours upon hours of the television series *Eyes on the Prize*, read Taylor Branch, and met with a few of the actual Freedom Riders living in Minnesota as part of our historical research. It was an honor to meet them and hear their stories. I was deeply inspired by the college students and young adults who had traveled interstate to challenge segregation and register Black voters in 1964. When the play opened, we did about six shows per week, which later prepared me for the rigors of professional theatre performance. The experience of creating art inspired by historical subject matter had a lasting impact on the creative work I pursue to this day.

My parents were supportive of my participation in the play, but surprisingly didn't offer their own stories, no matter how many questions I asked. On car rides home from rehearsal, I'd ask my mom, "Where were you during the summer of 1964?"

"Let's see, I was living in California with Aunt Bernice," she'd say with a shrug from behind the steering wheel.

"Well, what about Dad? Where was he?" I asked, begging for insights into their own personal freedom fight.

"Your dad was at Michigan State, I guess. We were in college, Maya," she'd respond with little animation, almost annoyed by my endless questions.

It was confusing and frustrating that in my gut I knew they had to have been impacted in some way by the events of 1964, but as a teenager, I didn't know what questions to ask. My parents were business executives active in corporate diversity and inclusion efforts, born out of the legislative gains of the 1960s, but in my 15-year-old brain, I concluded that they were completely absent from the civil rights movement because they were "at college." It was lost on me that they were living their own barrier-breaking stories.

A key moment of the Youth Performance Company production of *Freedom Riders* centered on the brutal murders of James Earl Chaney,

Andrew "Andy" Goodman, and Michael "Mickey" Schwerner in Neshoba County, Mississippi. I was most intrigued by the fact that the three men weren't much older than I was when they disappeared during the Freedom Summer of 1964. They were youth volunteers—one Black and two white—assigned to a statewide voter registration action coordinated by the Council of Federated Organizations (COFO) in Jackson, Mississippi, made up of national civil rights groups, namely the Student Nonviolent Coordinating Committee (SNCC), the Congress of Racial Equality (CORE), and the National Association for the Advancement of Colored People (NAACP).

Being cast in the show was a much-needed reprieve from my high school environment, which had grown even more stifling and suffocating than junior high school became after the "slavery" unit. Learning about the ways that northern white students from respectable families used their privilege to assist Black leaders in the South gave me perspective, and a longing to see that level of commitment to the advancement of race relations among my white peers. I couldn't imagine the white kids from my high school being as brave as the white and Jewish students from the North who descended upon the state of Mississippi throughout the summer of 1964. Nor could I imagine them having the courage to stand up to the local Ku Klux Klan. I'd never heard the story of Chaney, Goodman, and Schwerner before being cast in the play.

Klansmen planned and executed a plot to kill Mickey Schwerner and lured the three workers to investigate beatings and a church burning at Mount Zion Methodist Church near Philadelphia, Mississippi, on June 16, 1964. On their way back to Meridian, they were pulled over by Cecil Ray Price, a Neshoba County deputy and also a Klan member. He tracked their station wagon's plates to CORE and arrested them for speeding. They spent the night in jail and were released after paying a $20 fine. The three made national news when they didn't arrive in Meridian as scheduled. The FBI launched an investigation that led to the discovery of their bodies in an earthen dam on a farm in Neshoba

County on August 4, 1964, just as my dad was beginning his sophomore year at Michigan State.

Much like the violence that pervades the periphery of our day-to-day cultural experiences in the 21st century, people were still maintaining a shocking amount of normalcy nationwide in the shadows of the violence and death that surrounded them. Nineteen defendants were eventually indicted in the Klan conspiracy and cover-up of their murders in 1967, although at the time only eight were successfully convicted and prosecuted. The reopening of the case by the Department of Justice through the modern Emmett Till Unsolved Civil Rights Crime Act led to the conviction of Edgar Ray Killen, who was finally charged with manslaughter in 2005.

College football history and my dad's time at Michigan State are firmly situated in the racial climate of America during the 1960s. Mississippi was the site of endless suffering for Black Americans and those who dared to challenge white supremacy. However, the happenings in Neshoba County in the summer of 1964 didn't seem to interrupt the start of football season at the University of Mississippi or the rest of the country. A few hours' drive away from where the civil rights workers were slain, the Ole Miss Rebels started the season ranked first in the polls going into the fall. As we say in the theatre, *the show must go on*, and it did for college football—even as the United States of America was in the midst of a battle for its very soul.

Up in East Lansing, Michigan, the visibility of the Michigan State football program had the potential to further the doctrine of equal opportunity by recruiting Black players from the South. MSU president John A. Hannah continued to support Biggie Munn's Athletic Department as Duffy Daugherty expanded the recruitment pipeline and built what would eventually become the first fully integrated program in America based on numbers of Black players. Michigan State University's most significant move in 1964 was scouting a soft-spoken Black quarterback from Fayetteville, North Carolina.

Jimmy Raye started receiving letters from Michigan State and the University of Minnesota in 1964, his senior year of high school in segregated North Carolina. Like my dad, he was a standout athlete at his all-Black high school. Jimmy was voted Most Valuable Player in an East-West Shriners game for Black players in Durham, North Carolina, which caught the eye of Michigan State coach Cal Stoll, who presented the trophy. A friendly courting of Jimmy Raye began as the institution continually sent letters and questionnaires to Fayetteville, North Carolina, with plans for a visit. Then, out of nowhere, the communications came to an unexpected halt. For two months Jimmy Raye didn't hear from the Spartans, and he started to put his attention toward the historically Black colleges in the region who'd ramped up their recruitment efforts in his direction. Florida A&M, Tennessee State, Morgan State, and North Carolina A&T began to receive sincere consideration from Jimmy Raye as the weeks passed with no word from Michigan State.

As I was sitting across from Jimmy in the Kellogg Center, all mic'ed up for our interview in 2014, it was hard for me to believe that, with all he went on to accomplish as a college athlete and longtime coach in the NFL, Michigan State almost let this talented Black quarterback slip through their hands.

He proceeded to tell me how a childhood friend inspired him not to give up on the possibility of attending Michigan State. "So we were sitting around my house one day and my dear friend Ron Chalmers suggested, 'Why don't we write them a letter and find out if they are still interested.' So we sit down and we pen the letter and send it to Cal Stoll and Duffy. Fortunately for me, defensive coach Vince Carillot got the letter someway—I don't know how he got it, but they had given out all of the scholarships. One of the scholarships had been given out to a quarterback in Chicago, who decided to sign a pro baseball contract. So as luck would have it, my letter arrived the same time as the other guy gave back his commitment to Michigan State."

The Spartan coaches arranged for Jimmy to come up and take a trip to East Lansing, hosted by the friendly Black linebacker Charlie "Mad Dog" Thornhill from Roanoke, Virginia. Like my dad during his recruitment trip the year prior, Jimmy navigated the new integrated environment with bravery—and a few butterflies.

"I was supposed to meet Vince Carillot downstairs for breakfast. I got down there a little early and the lady hostess asked me if I wanted to come in and sit down and wait for him. I didn't know what to do because where I came from you couldn't go in the restaurant and sit down. So I sat there," Jimmy told me, with the same nervousness he'd had when he was fresh out of Fayetteville.

"She finally convinced me to sit down," he continued. "And I sat there filled with anxiety. I'm thinking someone's gonna tap me on my shoulder and ask me, 'What are you doing sitting in here?' and tell me to leave. Vince finally showed up for breakfast. I'm looking over the menu and talking to him, still thinking how was, you know, this going to work? He kind of helped me along. He said, 'Well, the blueberry pancakes here are outstanding and everybody, almost all other player recruits—they love the blueberry pancakes.' And so I said, 'Thank you,' and ordered the blueberry pancakes."

The nuances of entering an integrated world where Black students were in the minority challenged everyone involved. The Black players were expected to make a contribution in order to justify this experiment. Full integration of the MSU football team meant that the pressure to win was intense. The biggest concern for Jimmy Raye and his parents was whether or not he'd be able to achieve his academic goals and also be able to play quarterback. Michigan State and other schools in the Big Ten were attracting some of the best Black players in the country who otherwise might have attended historically Black colleges in the South, but Black quarterbacks were few and far between. At the time, Jimmy was aware of only a few African American quarterbacks at major schools throughout the North.

Sandy Stevens had made a name for himself at the University of Minnesota, and Willie Lee Thrower played at Michigan State on the 1952 National Championship team. Recruited by then *assistant* coach Duffy Daugherty, Willie made a contribution at MSU as the first African American quarterback in the Big Ten Conference, and later in the NFL as one of the first African American quarterbacks in the league, as well as the first to play in an NFL game. At the time, his accomplishments were met with little fanfare. Thrower's legacy was significant in opening doors for a Black quarterback like Jimmy Raye, but he wasn't a starter when he played for the Spartans. Inspired by Willie Thrower, but aware of the obstacles he'd faced for field time, Jimmy Raye wondered if he would be allowed to further his talents as a quarterback at Michigan State. This question weighed on his mind as he spent time visiting East Lansing with his host, Charlie "Mad Dog" Thornhill.

Getting to know the Black players on campus during his visit, he was encouraged by meeting fellow standouts like upperclassmen Jim Garrett and Bob Moreland, who made him feel welcome but warned that if he accepted the scholarship at Michigan State, he might have to change positions. They cited the fact that Eric Marshall, a Black quarterback from Oxford, Mississippi, had to switch positions when he got to Michigan State. There wasn't a precedent to guarantee that Jimmy would be able to stay in the quarterback position. He feared that Duffy Daugherty would bow to external pressures from those in the East Lansing community who held the belief that Black people didn't have the intellect to lead a team in the highly cerebral role of quarterback. White America was barely comfortable with Black linebackers crushing their white counterparts, or Black running backs outrunning the white defense. How could they fully embrace a Black quarterback? A Black *starting* quarterback?

As Daugherty's team became "Blacker," the optics alone spoke to intrinsic fears about what might happen if Black people gained a kind of liberation that allowed them to compete against all-white football teams and win. Whether or not Michigan State would be willing to give him a chance was a real concern as he continued with his campus visit. Meeting younger players like my dad, Jim Summers, George "Mickey" Webster, and Bubba Smith helped relieve some of his concerns because they seemed to carry a bit more optimism just off their first year of eligibility as sophomores.

The decision ultimately came down to getting his parents' blessing. The Black community in Fayetteville offered their two cents to the Raye family every chance they got. There was skepticism and concern surrounding his opportunity to play quarterback, and how sincere Michigan State was about supporting him academically. One of Duffy's former coaching assistants assigned to the North Carolina area, Earle Edwards, was now the head coach at North Carolina State University. Duffy likely persuaded Earle to contact Jimmy's parents in an attempt to encourage him to go to Michigan State. Coach Edwards understood the nuances of race and college recruiting. He assured the Raye family that Biggie Munn and Duffy Daugherty would offer their son a fair shot.

Coach Edwards had ascended to the role of head coach at North Carolina State, yet he worked for an institution that still upheld racial segregation. This is the paradox that *good* white people appear to encounter throughout history as they create a better life for themselves, even if it requires a hearty threshold for apathy in the face of the blatant discrimination Black Americans experience. While North Carolina State University had enrolled two Black graduate students, Robert Clemons and Hardy Liston, in 1953, and had four Black undergraduate students, Ed Carson, Manuel Crockett, Irwin Holmes, and Walter Holmes, in 1956, the school did not have a Black football player until 1967, when Marcus Martin arrived.

In the same breath that Coach Edwards participated in a power structure that discriminated against Jimmy (who he couldn't recruit at North Carolina State University for his own team even though it was mere miles away from Jimmy's hometown), he attempted to help him, or at least his former boss Duffy Daugherty, by persuading him to attend Michigan State.

When Jimmy's mother took a call from Duffy, she asked, "Will my boy be able to play quarterback?"

Duffy responded with gusto. "He'll be a quarterback until he decides he's not a quarterback."

With that, Jimmy's parents agreed to allow their son to take a 38-hour train ride to East Lansing and start his academic and athletic career at Michigan State University.

CHAPTER
TEN

The 1964 football season was the appointed time for the Black players who'd excelled at their all-Black high schools in the South. Jim Garrett from Columbia, South Carolina; Maurice Haynes from Baton Rouge, Louisiana; Ernie Pasteur from Beaufort, North Carolina; Bubba Smith from Beaumont, Texas; Jim Summers from Orangeburg, South Carolina; Charlie "Mad Dog" Thornhill from Roanoke, Virginia; Solomon Townsend from South Bend, Indiana; George "Mickey" Webster from Anderson, South Carolina; and my dad, Gene Washington, from La Porte, Texas, understood that going back to their segregated hometowns was not a viable option.

Led by quarterback Steve Juday, the MSU offense demonstrated their potential early in the season, winning against USC 17–7, and losing to North Carolina, Michigan, and Indiana, by seven points or less per game. The team wasn't getting much love from the press or even the pollsters, but a synergy was building. For the Black players from the South, proving themselves was at the forefront of their minds in the classroom and on the field. This was their one chance to receive an education at a major university. They knew that if they didn't excel, they'd be sent back to the South. They had to be their personal best and work as a team, but also fearless enough to stand out to secure victories for themselves and consequently *the race*. Making a significant contribution on the field was key to achieving a better life for themselves and their families.

The *New York Times* threw sportswriter shade at the team but gave my dad some love in its October 11, 1964, recap of the Michigan versus Michigan State game:

> Although the Spartan offense was mediocre, a sophomore end named Gene Washington stood out. He caught only one pass—a spectacular leaping grab for 43 yards—but he repeatedly outfoxed the Michigan secondary only to be overthrown. A three-time Texas high school champion in the high and low hurdles, Washington reminded one spectator of Del Shofner of the New York Giants with his ability to lope downfield, apply an almost imperceptible head fake, and burst into the open.

If he hadn't been the standout athlete that he was, I wonder if I'd be able to find these crouton-sized bread crumbs that help me piece together my father's life. It's unbelievable that my dad was being recognized so many miles away from La Porte, Texas, for his performance in a football game that his team *lost*.

One of the things my dad still expresses frustration about is the fact that the athletic achievements of the all-Black high schools in his region growing up were never recognized in the local papers. They received hand-me-down uniforms and often substandard equipment from the white schools. For my dad to find himself on the national stage, and his name in the *New York Times* as a sophomore, was a small glimpse into what was possible for him and other Black men from the South. The *New York Times* compared my *Black* dad to a *professional white wide receiver*, Del Shofner, from his home state of Texas. A state that was still very much segregated the whole time my father was in college.

Midseason, the defense started to come together, holding off opponents Northwestern, Wisconsin, and Purdue, but lost to Notre Dame (7–34) and Illinois (0–16) as the Spartans finished out the season 4–5 with a sixth-place ranking in the Big Ten Conference. Nationally, the Spartans ranked 20th, alongside Mississippi, in the UPI Coaches Poll. My dad and his *racially integrated* Spartan team sat at the bottom of the polls, tied with Mississippi's *all-white* team, as if the art of football was beginning to imitate the divide between those who took the 1954 *Brown v. Board of Education* ruling seriously, and those who upheld the racist traditions and customs of the past with all obstinate speed.

White citizens' councils promoting segregation and white supremacy among their constituents sprang up throughout the South after the *Brown v. Board of Education* ruling. They had one main obsession: to politically and economically thwart efforts to desegregate schools and public accommodations. In 1956, the Association of Citizens' Councils of Mississippi, a segregationist organization, was formed around their white supremacist philosophy. The association was a key factor in the election of governor Ross Barnett, a Dixiecrat who ran on a staunch segregationist platform in 1959.

Governor Barnett, the University of Mississippi, and the customs of white supremacy got 15 minutes of national infamy in 1962. It wasn't the Ole Miss Rebels undefeated team that caught everyone's attention that year, but the national crisis that unfolded when a Black student, James Meredith, attempted to register for classes in September.

President Kennedy, attorney general Robert Kennedy, and governor Ross Barnett were in weeks-long negotiations to provide a security plan to enroll James Meredith at Ole Miss. The John F. Kennedy Presidential Library contains correspondence and transcripts from phone calls between the parties focused on quelling

any possibility of violence. Based on the correspondence, it appears
that Barnett was playing both sides by appeasing Kennedy privately
in the phone calls, then defiantly making a public declaration of
war, sure to incite violence, which was broadcast on local radio and
television on September 13, 1962.

> I speak to you now in the moment of our greatest cri-
> sis since the War Between the States . . . I have said in
> every county in Mississippi that no school in our state will
> be integrated while I am your governor. I repeat to you
> tonight: no school in our state will be integrated while I
> am your governor. There is no case in history where the
> Caucasian race has survived social integration. We will not
> drink from the cup of genocide.

Thousands of white protesters responded to Governor Barnett's
rallying cry and descended on the Oxford, Mississippi, campus
and the surrounding community. On September 29, 1962, Barnett
attended the Ole Miss versus Kentucky football game. Halftime
featured the unfurling of Confederate flags on the field and in the
stands. He addressed the crowd, which was well aware that James
Meredith was attempting to enroll at Ole Miss, in yet another call-
to-arms speech: "I love Mississippi! I love her people, our customs. I
love and I respect our heritage."

Despite the fact that attorney general Robert Kennedy negotiated
with Governor Barnett for a peaceful plan for James Meredith to register
for classes, rioting mobs of white protestors—enraged by the idea of
a qualified 29-year-old Air Force veteran, who happened to be Black,
gaining successful enrollment to Ole Miss—erupted in deadly violence.
The venomous crowd of angry white people included students, community members, and those who'd traveled to Oxford from outside.

They cheered for Governor Barnett when he arrived at the Lyceum building, where the registration was scheduled to take place.

Throughout the weekend, local Black residents who weren't even involved in the James Meredith enrollment were harassed and beaten. Three hundred people were injured and two were killed on the Oxford campus. Marshals and National Guardsmen sent by President Kennedy to protect James Meredith and keep order were among the injured. After multiple attempts met by the physical obstruction of Governor Barnett and widespread violence on the campus, James Meredith was successfully escorted by federal marshals on October 1, 1962. After the deadly riots, a security detail was assigned to James Meredith for the duration of his education at the University of Mississippi. In the years that followed, intimidation, harassment, propaganda, and strategic social and economic oppression were the definitive playbook of tactics used to suppress and punish Black Americans attempting to vote, attend college, eat at restaurants, use the restroom, receive medical care, earn a living, and other basic expressions of human rights under the law. At the end of the 1964 season, Ole Miss, a segregated team, was tied with an integrated Michigan State team for number 20 in the polls. The State of Mississippi, however, was at the top of the leader board when it came to victims of racial violence after the 1954 *Brown v. Board of Education* ruling.

MISSISSIPPI MURDERS

1955

REVEREND GEORGE LEE
BELZONI, MS

A minister and head of the local NAACP. Shot in the face for refusing to withdraw his name from the town's qualified voter list, and for registering other Black people to vote.

EMMETT TILL
MONEY, MS

A child. Accused of flirting with a white shopkeeper. Kidnapped, beaten, shot in the head, and thrown in a river.

LAMAR SMITH
BROOKHAVEN, MS

An elder. Shot on the courthouse lawn for registering Black people to vote in a runoff election.

1959

MACK CHARLES PARKER
POPLARVILLE, MS

A 23-year-old truck driver accused of raping a white woman. Kidnapped, beaten, murdered by a mob, and thrown into a river, although multiple lie detector results were either inconclusive or supported his insistence of innocence.

1961

HERBERT LEE
LIBERTY, MS

A cotton and dairy farmer known to support Black voter registration. Shot in the head by a Mississippi state representative in a public setting.

1962

CORPORAL ROMAN DUCKSWORTH JR.
TAYLORSVILLE, MS

A father of five on emergency leave to attend to his wife as she gave birth to their sixth child. Fell asleep on the bus ride home. Struck in the head repeatedly with a blackjack and shot in the heart by a police officer.

PAUL GUIHARD
OXFORD, MS

French reporter covering James Meredith's enrollment at the University of Mississippi. Shot in the back during a riot targeting James Meredith and US marshals.

1963

MEDGAR EVERS
JACKSON, MS

Director of the NAACP and the campaign for racial integration. Shot in the back on the front steps of his home with his family inside.

1964

LOUIS ALLEN
LIBERTY, MS

Witness to the 1961 murder of
Herbert Lee. Harassed, assaulted,
and later shot in the face in his
driveway after telling the FBI and
the United States Commission
on Civil Rights what he saw.

HENRY HEZEKIAH DEE
CHARLES EDDIE MOORE
MEADVILLE, MS

A sawmill worker, and a college
student. Kidnapped, tortured,
and drowned by Klansmen.

JAMES EARL CHANEY
ANDREW GOODMAN
MICHAEL HENRY SCHWERNER
NESHOBA COUNTY, MS

Civil rights workers investigating
a church burning. Arrested for
speeding. Kidnapped, beaten,
and shot by Klansmen after
their release.

CHAPTER
ELEVEN

The Great Migration to northern cities began near the turn of the 20th century and continued throughout my parents' childhoods. This Black exodus later swept them up and off to lives outside of Texas when they came of age in the 1960s. After graduation from high school, my mother became part of a Black and Creole migration from the South to Northern and Southern California that began in the 1940s. A willingness to move toward a better life, even if it meant a physical change in geography, was critical to my ancestors' economic and cultural survival in the United States for generations. My mother's parents, Burnice and Lula Mae Goudeau, had eight children in all, five girls and three boys. My mother was the third youngest, born after they'd migrated with other families from Goudeau and Bunkie, Louisiana, not far from Evergreen where my dad's parents were from.

My grandfather built a humble house in McNair Station, a small Black and Creole enclave near Baytown, Texas. They didn't have indoor plumbing or other modern luxuries. Other relatives from Louisiana built homes in the community and lived walking distance from one another. As Louisiana Creoles, they descended from a people uniquely originating in the colonial Americas. By the 1940s and 1950s, Creole families like mine were mostly absorbed within the Black population

during Jim Crow. At the time, being "American" was about one's proximity to Anglo-American whiteness after the Louisiana Purchase in 1803.
For my mother and other Creole children of the time, they maneuvered
through the nuances of colorism that favored their fair skin, the result
of their mixed African, Native American, Spanish, and French blood,
all the while embracing their *Coloredness* and desire to fit in among their
Black classmates and neighbors.

In high school, my mother's sisters were voted Miss Carver for
their balance of beauty and brains. The duality of being admired for
your beauty but made fun of for your culture was a paradox they
took in stride. The kids would tease them and call them *gumbo heads*
and *crawfish eaters*. My grandparents and great-grandparents spoke a
French-Creole dialect but insisted that my mother and her siblings
speak English impeccably. The desire to assimilate and be accepted by
Americans was at the root of their understanding of survival. The idea
that they *were* as American as America could be—as the descendants
of the original indigenous North Americans, the Africans who were
brought here, and the French and Spanish who colonized and enslaved
them—was not on their minds when it came to how they moved in
the world. My great-grandmother considered herself French, and had a
love-hate relationship with *Americans* and *Americanness*.

While some Creoles were white-passing—meaning their skin, features, and hair made it easy to perceive them as white, so they lived their
lives as white people—my grandparents embraced the genetic variations
within themselves and their offspring. They lived proudly as Black, even
if it meant they would be treated as second-class citizens by whites, or
with suspicion and contempt from other Black people. In the family
photos and film I've seen of my mother's parents, my grandmother
Lula holds a seriousness in her gaze that I perceive as a bit of sadness
behind her cat-eye frames. My grandfather Burnice, on the other hand,
seems to wear a *good time guy* grin that likely tested Lula's patience
and relationship with God. Burnice's fair skin and eyes, his oil-slicked,

Clark Kent wavy side part, and his simple white shirt and slacks are like the men I'd seen in old black-and-white movies and TV shows as a kid. He worked as a handyman and also in the oil refineries, while my grandmother was a homemaker. Aside from my mother's horrifying memories of riding in my grandfather's pickup truck after he'd had too much to drink, most everyone talks about what a great guy Burnice Goudeau was.

He provided for the family and used whatever relationships he'd built in town to purchase goods at the downtown shops. My aunt Arvia remembers he'd measure the children's feet at home with a string, then bring the string into the store and have the shopkeeper find shoes that were the equivalent length. My aunt found it annoying because their shoes never fit right. She didn't understand why they couldn't try on the shoes in the store to make sure they fit before he brought them home. Black folks and light- to brown-skinned Creoles found ways to maneuver in a segregated society to address the basic needs of their families. Rather than subject small children to the potential dangers of stepping out of line in the presence of white people, my grandparents used creativity and ingenuity to shield my mother and her siblings from racism as best they could.

My grandparents instilled the value of self-reliance and displayed a commitment to the community in response to the conditions they were forced to endure under Jim Crow. My grandmother would always make extra food and have my mom and her siblings bring things to their relatives and neighbors who lived in the community. If a student didn't have money for a uniform or a participation fee for extracurricular activities, others in the community would pitch in to take care of them. My parents' courtship actually began while they were studying at my grandparents' kitchen table as classmates. The familiarity and willingness to open their homes to others was a matter of hospitality but also an important stabilizing belief system that supported the Black community. So, when my mom graduated from George Washington

Carver High School, it was only natural that her sisters supported her move to Northern California to pursue her education at San Francisco State and later Contra Costa College.

Her sisters Bernice and Arvia had left McNair Station, Texas, as married women a few years earlier, and my mom leaped at the opportunity to experience life outside of Jim Crow. When she arrived, she soon realized that opportunities for education and employment were indeed better for people of color in California than they had been in Texas, yet my mother and her sisters still lived humbly as they fashioned a life in the Bay Area. My aunt Bernice helped my mother get a job working part time at MJB Coffee Company, starting off as a file clerk. She was later promoted to accounting clerk, which allowed her to save quite a bit of money. This was great fortune for my mother because Black people faced housing and employment discrimination, even in California at the time. One cost-saving technique she employed was sharing a wardrobe. My aunt Bernice would wear a work dress on Monday, then my mom would wear the same dress on Tuesday. My mom helped her sisters with the minutiae of raising their small children and spent time at both households in San Francisco and Richmond. She kept up a correspondence with my dad through letters and the occasional long distance phone call from him.

Unlike my father, who was extremely isolated in Michigan, my mother was enveloped in the goings-on of the student movements from 1963 to 1966 at nearby Berkeley. While filming the documentary, I enjoyed hearing about my mom's experiences. She can be an emotional live wire at times, so the gift of having the camera and sound crew in the room during our interviews offered a much more objective view of her life—something I'd never likely experience over a cup of tea at the kitchen table. Sitting under the lights in my parents' formal living room, we were able to go back in time to her college days together as she spoke about those early experiences.

Gene and Maya dance at a community event in Minneapolis, Minnesota.
Courtesy of the author.

Above: Bobby Marshall (middle row, on the left) and his teammates on the Central High School baseball team in 1900 in Minneapolis.
Courtesy of Hennepin History Museum.

Below: Jack Trice in his Iowa State University football uniform in 1923.
Courtesy of Iowa State University Library, University Archives.

Above: Michigan Agricultural College varsity football team in 1913.

*Below: Gideon Smith, the first Black football player at
Michigan Agricultural College, circa 1914.*
Images courtesy of Michigan State University Archives
and Historical Collections.

President John F. Kennedy meets with members of the U.S.
Commission on Civil Rights in the Oval Office. From left to right:
Dr. John A. Hannah, Erwin N. Griswold, and Berl I. Bernhard.
Courtesy of Abbie Rowe. White House Photographs.
John F. Kennedy Presidential Library and Museum, Boston.

Above: Dr. John A. Hannah arrives in Lexington, Kentucky, on November 1, 1946, for the University of Kentucky–Michigan State football game. He is accompanied by (from left to right) tackle Alger Conner, halfback Russ Reader, and head coach Charles W. Bachman.
Courtesy of University of Kentucky Libraries Special Collections Research Center.

Below: Horace Smith, All-American running back for Michigan State College.
Courtesy of a private collection.

Head coach Duffy Daugherty and defensive coach
Henry "Hank" Bullough discuss football plays in 1968.
Courtesy of Michigan State University Archives and Historical Collections.

Above: Gene with his parents, Henry and Alberta Washington.

Below: Recruiter and Michigan State coach Cal Stoll
with Gene Washington in Spartan Stadium.
Images courtesy of the author.

Above: Gene Washington.

Below: Bubba Smith.

Images courtesy of Michigan State University Archives
and Historical Collections.

Above: US president Lyndon B. Johnson signs the Civil Rights Act, with Martin Luther King Jr. in attendance, on July 2, 1964.
White House Photo / Alamy Stock Photo.

Middle: FBI notice seeking information about the disappearance of civil rights workers Andrew Goodman, James Earl Chaney, and Michael Henry Schwerner, who were abducted and murdered by Ku Klux Klan members.
FLHC 1C / Alamy Stock Photo.

Below: Flanked by US marshals, James Meredith walks to class at the University of Mississippi. In 1962, he became the first African American student admitted to the segregated school.
American Photo Archive / Alamy Stock Photo.

Gene Washington, George Webster, Clinton Jones, Charlie Thornhill,
and Bubba Smith receive UPI All-America recognition.
Courtesy of the author.

Above: Gene Washington makes a leaping grab in Spartan Stadium.
Courtesy of Michigan State University Archives and Historical Collections.

Below: Gene Washington wins first place at a track meet.
Courtesy of the author.

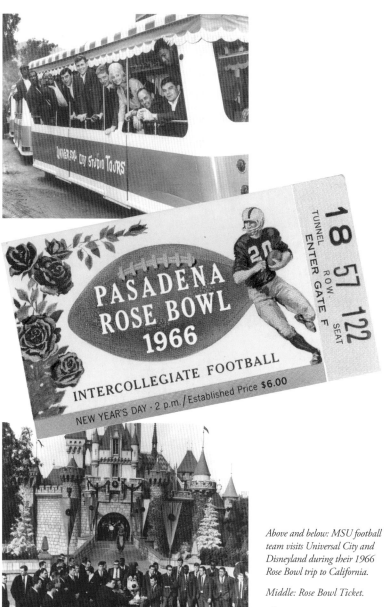

Above and below: MSU football team visits Universal City and Disneyland during their 1966 Rose Bowl trip to California.

Middle: Rose Bowl Ticket.

All images courtesy of Michigan State University Archives and Historical Collections.

Above: Scoreboard at the "Game of the Century," November 19, 1966.
Courtesy of Michigan State University Archives and Historical Collections.

Below: George Webster, Clinton Jones (front), Charlie Thornhill,
Jeff Richardson and Larry Lukasik (back) before the "Game of the
Century" against Notre Dame.
Photo by Bob Gomel/The LIFE Premium Collection via Shutterstock.

Above: Gene and Claudith Washington, wedding photo, June 17, 1967.

Below: Vikings newsletter article, "The Woman Behind the Man," still photo clipping; original caption: "Claudith Washington, left, with Yvette Winston in their seats at a Vikings game to cheer for their husbands."
Images courtesy of the author.

Above: NFL Championship: Minnesota Viking Gene Washington makes a
catch against the Cleveland Browns at Metropolitan Stadium.
Photo by Walter Iooss Jr / *Sports Illustrated* via Getty Images.

Below: Gene Washington, wearing number 84 for the Broncos in 1973, catches
a 20-yard pass in the end zone in a game vs. the San Diego Chargers.
Photo by John Beard / *The Denver Post* via Getty Images.

Above: Gene, Maya, and Clinton tour the U.S. Bank Stadium.
Courtesy of Minnesota Vikings and the author.

Below: Greg Coleman jokes with Gene Washington, Bud Grant, and
Clinton Jones at the Minnesota Vikings Training Facility during the panel
discussion after a screening of Through the Banks of the Red Cedar.
Courtesy of the author.

"It was freeing, because I was in an environment with so many different kinds of people from Australia, the Philippines, Mexico, even Chile. And there was a new freedom where it was safe to talk about things that bothered you. And also to find hope. You didn't have to stay mired in the society that held you back," she explained.

In that moment during our interview, I realized how much early exposure to international perspectives shaped who she was as a young woman, and in turn, how she raised her children. Many of my parents' friends were from all around the world when I was growing up. My mother is fluent in French and Spanish and encouraged my sisters and me to speak both languages at home. Having the opportunity to ask my mom more about the political climate was a first in terms of my being able to understand who she was in her late teens and early 20s.

"Were you aware of Martin Luther King or others working on civil rights issues?" I asked, grateful that a portal to who she was opened between us.

"I was very active in our college politics," she asserted. "Dr. King came to our college and spoke. I was on a lot of committees at our school while your dad was at Michigan State. In the '60s we had Stokely Carmichael, Angela Davis, and all those people—I was right in the middle of that—Mario Savio and Free Speech . . . those were the people that were drumming things into my psyche."

What in the world? I thought as the cameras continued to roll. I was definitely hearing all of this for the first time. I learned about the Black and brown political figureheads of the '60s on my own accord. I had no idea that my mother was in the thick of so much history as a young woman. The only time I heard the words "Angela Davis" was when my mother described the Afro her youngest sister, Lynette, wore throughout college. The style was affectionately referred to as an *Angela Davis* within the Black community at the time. The only other memory I have connected to my mother and Aunt Lynette's affection for the Black Panthers was the story of how they put my mother's Afro wig on my sister Lisa and trained her to throw up her little fist and say, "Black Power," as a toddler. The words falling out of her little mouth sounded more like Black *powder* than *power,* so it was a favorite story they liked to tell.

In contrast to my dad and his teammates at Michigan State, whose exposure to the movement was limited to a few campus speakers, like Martin Luther King Jr., my mom had the freedom to awaken to and exercise the ideas of Black American Liberation. "I remember participating in a protest when Governor Reagan was going to raise tuition in California. And so, a group of students were protesting peacefully, but on the evening news, the report focused on a rebel crowd that was acting up. Remember I was from Texas, you know, you kind of believed everything that was on television. But it was so negative, I thought, 'Oh my goodness, everything on television is not true.' That small group of people had been featured to discredit the whole purpose of the protest, and it was really about us poor students who couldn't afford the increase. We wouldn't have the money to go on to Berkeley and all these other places if they continued to raise tuition. That message was lost."

To say that SNCC, the NAACP, CORE, UC Berkeley's SLATE, the Black Panthers, and other visible young Black Americans speaking out against oppression had an impact on my parents and others nationwide is an understatement. For my mother, who came from small-town Jim Crow, these progressive voices shaped her understanding about the possibility of asserting one's right to do something about the hate-fueled violence and discrimination that Black people experienced in the US.

"It became okay to talk about it. It's almost as if once you acknowledge the truth, it becomes bigger. It became like a monster. We would hear stories of all the things that were done to Black people. And they always came as a warning. But to have the power behind you to say, *This is not right?* This should not be happening to any Black child, any Black person, *anybody.* And the empowerment, that's what was different. It wasn't the fact that we knew about it, but the sense of indignation that *we have a right* to be indignant and to do something about it. My dad had to go through hell as a worker in the oil refinery. We heard stories every day about somebody calling somebody a *nigger* or being denied a job—we knew all of that stuff. But to be able to say that you had a right to protest inequality? That was a whole new level, and it was scary," she explained.

The groundswell of resistance and protest occurred in the midst of turbulence and violence nationwide as young people asserted their rights as citizens. On February 21, 1965, Malcolm X was assassinated. Two weeks later, on March 7, 1965, known as "Bloody Sunday," Black men, women, and teenagers were beaten and trampled mercilessly by white police officers on foot and horseback, as they attempted to register to vote in Selma, Alabama. The brutal images were captured by journalists and broadcast on television. Similar to events in Mississippi in 1962 when James Meredith attempted to enroll in Ole Miss, it took federal protection from the National Guard to bring what eventually became the famous Selma to Montgomery March to a hard-won conclusion weeks later.

It's important to acknowledge those who were on the front lines of sacrifice for the liberation of themselves and others, but for every famous Black activist, there were countless unknown Black men and women overcoming economic injustice in their everyday lives. My mom was coming of age in what would become a new America, balancing work, school, and taking care of nieces and nephews to earn her keep. Her role in the movement at that time was self-preservation for herself and her loved ones. Knowing that she went on to a successful career in human resources for major corporations puts a lot into perspective for me. At that time, my mom didn't have much of a social life outside of her family. As hard as it was to pull her weight in her sisters' homes, earn a living, and save money, she enjoyed every minute.

"I felt like I was making progress. For the first time in my life I had a job—first time in my life I was making my own money, and learning how to budget," she said with a joyful lilt.

When it comes to my parents' long-distance relationship, my mother swears they were just *friends*, but my dad always perceived her as his high school sweetheart. On their phone calls and in letters, they talked about the difficulties they faced in the classroom and my dad's football and track events. She was able to keep up with Michigan State through his letters and the newspaper articles covering the team as it ascended to national prominence in 1965. One of my dad's classmates at Michigan State compiled an album full of articles and sent it to my mom in California so she could keep up with the team.

There was definitely a lot to keep up with. The 1965 Spartan football season opened at Spartan Stadium against UCLA on September 18, 1965. The defense held the Bruins to 3 points and the offense scored a respectable 13 points—these details became particularly significant by the end of the season. After all, the Bruins had snagged a Black running back, Mel Farr, from Bubba Smith's hometown, Beaumont, Texas. According to my dad, the Smith family made an introduction to Michigan State and Mel Farr was set to join him and Bubba in the 1963 recruit class. UCLA made a more spectacular offer and landed what would become the future NFL Offensive Rookie of the Year.

While Mel Farr was doing his thing at UCLA, Bubba Smith was capturing the hearts of all of East Lansing on and off the field. The stands would erupt in cheers and chants of "Kill, Bubba, kill!" The giant from Beaumont, Texas, was never at a loss for attention. He took his growing fame in stride. His bravado was a staple at practice, where he regularly butted heads with the coaching staff and occasionally teammates. Nevertheless, it was clear that Duffy Daugherty's aggressive recruitment of southern Black players was paying off. With every win on their primarily Big Ten Conference schedule, the Spartans rose to national prominence in all of the polls by their seventh game against Northwestern. They blew the Wildcats out of the stadium 49–7.

In just a few weeks, the 1965 Spartan defense grew formidable. My dad's teammate Pat Gallinagh played tackle and was known as the 1965 and 1966 team poet laureate. Now in his 70s, he's a passionate man whose deep blue eyes cause the melody of the song "When Irish Eyes Are Smiling" to spontaneously dance around in my head.

Throughout my inquiry into the team history, he quickly became one of my staunchest supporters. His passion for the team and history poured out of him as he reflected on the moment he realized the team was truly great.

"You know there's an intangible in sports that's called *chemistry*, and it's like in marriage and in anything else, if it's there? It's there. I don't think anybody can really plant that," he said with a curious smile, trying to make sense of how well the team worked together.

"When did you know you were *great*?" I asked.

"We went out to Penn State and we were kind of—actually kind of scared. They were really built to be a powerhouse team but we shut them out 23–0. At that particular point in time, we began to think *maybe we're going to be good*. I think it really came home for us when we beat Purdue. We came back from a 10–0 deficit in the second half in West Lafayette and beat them. Then we knew we were for real. That was a mark of a great football team."

Out of nowhere, Duffy's Spartans became a powerhouse team with a notable amount of melanin taking the field in starting positions. I was curious about what my dad's white teammates thought about the ways they were completely upending the face of American college football, so I pressed Pat Gallinagh a bit.

"Were you aware of the racial climate at the time? Or how the fight against segregation impacted your teammates?" I asked.

"We were referred to sometimes as the 'Grambling of the North' because we had Black players on the field. I went back and looked at all the team pictures—you can literally count on one hand the number of African Americans there. Problem was for some people, they were all great athletes and they were all starters. So it looked like there was an awful lot more on the team than there were," he said with a shrug.

"What was it about Duffy that made him more open to giving Black players from the South or Pacific Islanders from Hawaii a shot?" I asked.

"He was an Irishman. Few people remember—and I'm a full-blooded Irishman—few people remember the time in America where there were signs all over that said, *No Irish Need Apply.* Duffy knew that history, so as Irish people, we were sensitive to people who were being discriminated against," he explained.

I enjoyed my sit-down with Pat Gallinagh and my dad's other white teammates. I found them to be more comfortable talking about race than my white classmates growing up in the '80s and '90s, and even my white co-workers and colleagues as an adult. So much so that when I asked about racial conflict on the team, neither the white nor the Black players had any significant events to report. Most of their difficulties around race came from the outside.

At first I thought they must have been in denial when they suggested there weren't any "race problems" on the team. My life in predominantly white environments was always wrought with tension and anxiety for me—I never quite knew where my classmates or teachers stood until something racial emerged, like being called a *nigger*, for example. So it was hard for me to believe things were so simple for my dad and his teammates. What I uncovered was that their interactions with one another existed in relation to white supremacist ideologies in practice in America at the time. The white players were from working-class families that had faced economic hardships, or worse if they came from less acceptable backgrounds, like Pat and Duffy's Irish heritage. They'd experienced limitations in their own lives, and at least among those I talked to, didn't have personal bias toward or hatred of their Black and Hawaiian teammates. Still, their interactions with my dad and other Black players from the South became an awakening to race-based disparities. This was especially true for Pat Gallinagh.

"The first time I ever met George 'Mickey' Webster was right here in the Kellogg Center where we are talking right now. Both of us were being recruited. He didn't know me. I didn't know him. The coaches were taking us around—introduced us—and I shook hands with him and he went his way and I went my way. It didn't make a big impression on me except Vince Carillot, one of our coaches, said something that stuck with me the rest of my life. He said, 'That might be the first time he ever shook hands with a white kid, and he's from Anderson, South Carolina. Down there—they had rules. If you violated them, you took your life in your hands literally, not just figuratively.' And so that has stuck with me. Detroit wasn't exactly a bastion of racial harmony. Where I was from we had de facto segregation there and the suburbs were mostly lily white, but we never had a case where we couldn't shake hands with somebody, or couldn't share a bus with them. They couldn't even sit at lunch counters in some places south of the Mason-Dixon. So that was the first time that discrimination ever really kind of hit home that way, and so that has stuck with me ever since."

The theory that Black people, white people, and native Hawaiians could play together in starting positions was tested on the banks of the Red Cedar River and everywhere the team played. Those who've studied the Spartans' 1965 and 1966 teams and their stats generally agree that the Spartan defense during those years was one of the best in college football history. Kids who grew up in East Lansing during that time frame recall going to Spartan Stadium and watching the historic games unfold. Sports journalist and historian Jack Ebling grew up watching the Spartans as a kid in East Lansing. He became a great source of information, and it helped that he's extremely passionate about this chapter in sports history.

"The '65 team and the tremendous defense, I think the greatest defense in college football history. They play Ohio State minus 22 yards rushing. Michigan? Minus 38 yards rushing. Notre Dame—minus 12 yards rushing. This wasn't just another Notre Dame team. This was a Notre Dame team that was ranked number four in the country. Michigan State ranked number one in the country," he said with a glint in his eye.

As I dug into the records for the 1965 team, I came to know that everything I'd heard or read about my dad and his teammates' playing ability was true. Clinton Jones, my dad's fellow track teammate and Bobbsey Twin, was a bold standout, scoring 12 touchdowns that season. His stats have him rushing for 787 yards, receiving for 308, with 65 kickoff returns, and a total of 1,160 yards. He even captured the Cleveland Touchdown Club's award for Most Outstanding College Player and Big Ten Conference Scoring Champion recognition. My dad was close behind him in the split end position with 40 receptions, 638 receiving yards, and 4 touchdowns. Their performance landed them on the All-Big Ten team honor rolls. My dad, Clinton Jones, Bubba Smith, George Webster, Steve Juday, Ron Goovert, Don Japinga, and Harold Lucas made First Team All-Big Ten. Their teammates John Karpinski, Bob Apisa, Jerry West, and Boris Dimitroff made Second Team. My dad, Bubba, and George Webster even made an appearance on *The Ed Sullivan Show* as members of the All-America team.

The most striking addition to the 1965 Spartans' racial integration story was quarterback Jimmy Raye. Even though Duffy faced opposition from acquaintances in East Lansing who objected to the mere idea of him starting a Black quarterback, Duffy delivered on the promise he made to Jimmy's mother during the recruitment process in 1964. Her son would play as a backup quarterback to senior and team MVP Steve Juday (who would finish sixth in the Heisman). The formidable defense held Michigan, Ohio State, and Notre Dame to manage total offense. The polls took notice of the undeniable power of Daugherty's team as the Spartans galloped toward a well-earned appearance in the 1966 Rose Bowl.

A trip to Pasadena meant that my mother, who was only a few hours away in the Bay Area, could travel down to Southern California to watch the excitement unfold. The press began to refer to my dad and his teammates as the "Jolly Green Giants." When they arrived in Southern California for the Rose Bowl, Duffy's team descended from the belly of the plane wearing matching blazers. Their fresh haircuts saluting the late December sun were met by reporters and Rose Court queens greeting them at the base of the airstairs.

"They had us at Lawry's The Prime Rib and Disneyland—Whiskey a Go Go, Sunset Strip, and Lou Rawls. I mean, we were having a great time, and Bubb had a fraternity brother at UCLA who made sure that we got into all the parties," Jimmy Raye remembered with a smile.

And party they did. As a last-ditch effort to corral the enthusiasm and shield the team from the press and chaos surrounding the game, Duffy had the team sequestered at a monastery up in the mountains. The goal was to help the team focus in an environment removed from all of the Rose Bowl hoopla.

I'm fairly certain that I woke up to the Rose Parade on our family television set every New Year's Day throughout my formative years. I'm completely certain that I missed all of the USC versus UCLA football games that occurred at the Rose Bowl stadium the entire time I was at college. My dad's Rose Bowl ring and matching Rose Bowl watch were among the collection of jewelry and lapel pins he kept in a dish in his office den next to the paper clips and staplers. I had no appreciation for what an achievement going to the Rose Bowl was for my dad and his teammates. The accomplishment was always sitting right there when I used the family computer to type my term papers throughout high school.

In 2013, I had a chance to at least attempt to imagine what it was like for my dad's 1965 team and their successes as I followed the Spartan football team's momentum with him. It seemed as if my newfound interest in football coincided with one of the most exciting seasons in Spartan history since the 1960s. In December, we were invited to the Big Ten Conference Championship where my dad received the Ford-Kinnick Leadership Award during the game. The excitement of the Spartans taking on Ohio State and standing on the field as my dad received the award was—to this day—indescribable.

In the Black community, we often describe these moments for our elders as *getting their flowers while they're still living.* My dad seems to be in awe of every acknowledgment he receives in this last quarter of his life.

"It's good to be remembered," he said to me as we hauled the heavy glass trophy that was presented by Big Ten commissioner Jim Delany back to our suite to watch the rest of the game. It was a nerve-wracking showdown in Lucas Oil Stadium. The Spartans were up 17–0 before Ohio State scored 24 unanswered points to hold the lead into the fourth quarter. Thanks to some excellent defense and running, the Spartans scored 17 unanswered points of their own. The Spartans pulled out a victory with a final score of 34–24, which secured a place for the team in the 2014 Rose Bowl. The energy in the stadium was electric as my parents and I found ourselves swept up in the confetti and celebration on the field after the game. It was surreal to think that almost 50 years prior, before there was an actual Big Ten Championship game, my dad and his teammates had their own journey to the Rose Bowl. For the first time, I came to appreciate what a defining moment making the trip to Pasadena for the Rose Bowl was for my dad and his college teammates.

When my dad and the Spartans ran onto the field in the Rose Bowl on New Year's Day in 1966, the odds were stacked in their favor. They had the collective hopes of all of East Lansing behind them, and students and alumni both traveled to California to support the Spartan appearance in the Tournament of Roses. The team's confidence was further boosted by an undefeated record and that season opening win

13–3 against running back Mel Farr and the UCLA Bruins. This was a rematch at best, and the Spartans and everyone else believed they were assured victory. My mother spent the pregame festivities with the coaches' families and took in the excitement. Her dear friend Eugene and his team were about to make history, and she was in the stands to witness it.

It wasn't long before a series of unfortunate events unfolded that no one—including the Spartans—saw coming. The Spartans failed to score throughout the first half of the game. UCLA made some long plays, led by Mel Farr and Gary Beban, who eventually won a Heisman Trophy in 1967. The Spartans' kicker, Dick Kenney, attempted a field goal at the 23-yard line but missed. Steve Juday, the Spartans' star quarterback, had a rough go of it. He struggled throughout the game, and by the fourth quarter, the Spartans were behind 14–0.

Jimmy Raye's heart raced as he watched Steve Juday struggle from the sidelines. He couldn't help wondering if Duffy would give him a chance to relieve him as quarterback. He'd done well as a backup throughout the season but wasn't sure if Duffy would give him a shot in such a high-profile moment for the team and the university.

"It was very difficult for me," Jimmy remembered as if he were reliving the experience. "I was the backup quarterback, and had played good all season, and played extremely well in a supportive role to Steve Juday. It was one of those days as quarterback that you have—and he had one—that we like to all soon forget. Duffy called me to warm up to go in the game because Steve was still struggling. He called to me and I started warming up on three different occasions, but he didn't put me in."

This continued to halftime and the Spartans were still down 14–0. Jimmy Raye looked to Duffy for the signal, but it didn't come. Years later, Jimmy would face similar scenarios from the perspective of a college and NFL coach, but as a young man on the field at that moment, he couldn't understand Duffy's hesitation in putting him in the game.

Jimmy was ready, willing, and he felt—*very much*—able to help the team.

"We're going to start you the second half and see if we can kick-start and go offensively," Duffy explained to the eager Jimmy Raye at halftime.

The team was playing well defensively, but the second half of the game required that they score their way to the win. As the team started back out onto the field after halftime, Duffy pulled Jimmy aside once again and said, "I know I told you we'll start you second half, but I'm going to give Steve one more series and see if he can get it going." He put his hand on Jimmy's shoulder and said, "I know you don't understand it now but you will."

This hesitation didn't make sense to Jimmy Raye, who was 19 years old and eager to contribute. He saw his elder teammate struggling and wanted to help the team. Duffy Daugherty's son, Danny, offered up an explanation for his dad's decision to hold off on putting Jimmy in the game, saying, "Steve Juday was his starting quarterback the entire season and All-American; he wasn't going to embarrass him on national television by benching him."

Duffy's concern for the reputation of his starting quarterback didn't prove beneficial in those first few series after halftime. In the fourth quarter, Steve Juday completed a 42-yard pass to my dad, but a comeback seemed to hang in the balance as the clock neared the final minutes of the game. Jimmy Raye watched series after series with adrenaline, until finally with six minutes to go, Duffy gestured to him and said, "Go."

The Spartans alternated between Juday and Raye in the final drives.

"I went out and hit Gene with a crucial third-down pass," Jimmy explained. "Made a pitch to Bob Apisa, and he went and he scored. And then we made a tremendous mistake after the first score. We went for two. I think we were caught up in winning the game as opposed to logically getting back in the game. We went for two and didn't make it, which meant that if we scored again, we had to go for two."

Steve Juday made completions to running back Dwight Lee, and later fullback Eddie Cotton, to the one-yard line. Juday then scored again to make it 14–12. With mere seconds left, the Spartans had to go for the two-point conversion in order to tie the game.

As Jimmy Raye told it, the Spartans called time-out. Duffy brought Jimmy Raye to the boundary and said, "I want you to tell the official to put the ball in the left hash mark, and we are going to run *spread option at nine.*"

"Okay, I got it," Jimmy Raye answered.

Duffy said, "Whatever you do, pitch the ball to Bob Apisa."

"Okay," Jimmy responded and started onto the field.

Duffy pulled him back and repeated emphatically, "Did you hear what I said? Whatever you do, pitch the ball to Bob."

"Okay, I got it," Jimmy replied, running back onto the field.

The directive made sense to Jimmy because of Bob's size. He figured that if he pitched the ball from two yards, all 235 pounds of Bob Apisa was going to go in. Jimmy told the official to move the ball to the left hash. The Spartans ran spread option at nine.

Jimmy sensed that the Bruins knew what was coming. "I mean, they knew what we were going to do," he said. "Move the ball to the right field. But we were still stoked—believed we'd get it in."

Jimmy Raye pitched the ball to Bob Apisa, and the Bruins defensive back Bobby Stiles plowed into the Hawaiian fullback, stopping him a yard short of the goal. The thing that Duffy and Jimmy didn't factor into what would otherwise have been a great game-tying play was the fact that Bob Apisa's bad knee would collapse under the weight of Bobby Stiles, who knocked himself unconscious to secure the win for the Bruins.

"I always felt—my dad was there at the game—and I knew, I could have run all the way home to Fayetteville from Pasadena with that ball inside if I didn't pitch it. I mean there was a cavity there that was as wide as the San Gabriel Mountains. But I was a good soldier. I pitched it to Bob and we lost the game 14–12. It was one of the most disappointing evenings I think I've ever experienced in football," Jimmy lamented.

All those years later, I could still feel the tension he must have experienced as a young man. I marveled at how he'd carried the weight of such a historical moment for almost 50 years.

"How did it feel second-guessing your instinct to run, but you did what your coach told you to do and pitched the ball?" I asked with as much respect as I could muster while picking my jaw up off the floor.

"Because I understood from the bond that we had as a team, and the selflessness that the players had. It wasn't as much about me as it was about the team. And this was about the team. Bob was 235 pounds and the orders, the marching orders, were to pitch. To defy that would have been—just wouldn't have been possible to deal with. I was given direct instructions on what to do, and to carry those out, and I did. I was able to live with that because I love Bob dearly, and he carried that burden with him for a long time, thinking that he failed us because he didn't make it in. His knee was bad and we were running to the right—he had more power off his good knee. I would say 9 out of 10 times he would have scored, and we would have tied the game."

I admire the way my dad and his teammates hold a lot of respect for one another over 50 years later. Steve Juday has become one of those kind faces that greet my dad and me when we visit East Lansing or other parts of Michigan with our documentary, *Through the Banks of the Red Cedar*. As hard as it must have been for Jimmy Raye to feel like he was being held back from contributing all those years ago, it's clear that he has great respect for Steve Juday and his team.

"He just had one of those days. When Duffy told me I would understand someday, it was true. When you get to senior year, you've paid the price to get to that point, and you were deserving of certain things because you have paid the debt, and that was Steve's opportunity.

I didn't understand it then, but as I grew in football and in athletics, I understood that. You got to let the guy have that. And that's what Duffy was trying to say to me: *It's Steve Juday's time and his moment and you'll have yours.* Steve and I have been friends for a lot of years, and we never really discussed or talked about it, and we don't have to because we both understand and know what was required of the position and what it meant," he said with resolve.

The Spartans did their best to hold their heads up as they left the stadium, knowing they'd be returning to disappointed fans back in East Lansing. As they boarded the plane home to Michigan, in a parallel but still segregated universe, the news reports announced that Alabama won its Orange Bowl match against Nebraska, catapulting the Crimson Tide to the post-season AP Poll's number-one spot as the 1965 National Champions. Michigan State maintained its number-one ranking with the UPI, FWAA, NFF, Helms, and other polls, making the Spartans Consensus National Champions alongside Alabama.

The thing that severely complicates the Consensus National Champions title for me is the fact that Alabama head coach Bear Bryant and Duffy Daugherty were "friends," but the possibility of the fully integrated Spartans having an opportunity to go head to head on the football field with the all-white Crimson Tide, in a state that had been resisting integration since Rosa Parks refused to sit in the back of a Montgomery bus in 1955, was nonexistent. Symbolically the two teams represented both America's segregated status quo and its integrated future as the nation's two National Champion teams in 1965.

CHAPTER

TWELVE

My dad and his Black teammates from the South survived multiple winters on a diet void of black-eyed peas, cornbread, and other soul foods, and became big men on campus by the end of 1965. Duffy Daugherty's recruitment experiment paid off dramatically and brought the Spartan football program back to national prominence. The team's success mirrored the political gains of the Johnson administration and MSU president John A. Hannah's Commission on Civil Rights in the form of the Voting Rights Act of 1965, alleviating some of the legal challenges for Black people from the South to participate in American democracy.

Literacy tests, poll taxes, and other bureaucratic requirements used to restrict Black voters were made illegal. Additionally, affirmative action received a boost when president Lyndon Johnson issued Executive Order 11246 on September 24, 1965 to enforce equal employment opportunities. It required government contractors to "take affirmative action" toward prospective minority employees in all aspects of hiring and employment. This represented the first time the phrase *affirmative action* entered the federal contracting lexicon to ensure employment equality. Eventually, Presidential Executive Order 11375 extended this language to include women on October 13, 1967.

Full participation in American democracy through the vote and an emphasis on leveling the economic playing field to gain employment previously denied to my parents and other protected groups were critical gains that had an impact on what's been possible for me as a Black woman years later. It meant that my dad, as a 21-year-old Black man, could work on the Oldsmobile factory line in Lansing during the summer to earn extra money alongside white workers. Back in Texas, the school districts in my parents' hometowns were still in the process of figuring out how to desegregate the schools, and their younger siblings were guinea pigs in the experiment.

Michigan State was very much a living—albeit isolated—laboratory. If Duffy Daugherty, the wealthy whites in the East Lansing community, and their middle-class and blue-collar counterparts didn't love Michigan State athletics as much as they did, this integration experiment could have ended badly—or worse, not existed at all. In many ways, my dad was protected by a cover of whiteness at the highest level with John A. Hannah as the university's president, reporting directly to President Kennedy and later President Johnson, throughout his college years.

When Bubba, my dad, and other Black players from the South went home to visit their families, those protections weren't there. Their hometowns were still segregated, which meant interstate travel was still risky—whether it involved a flight home (which many couldn't afford) or a train ticket where they'd have to ride in a *Colored* passenger car. My dad feels passionately about how the idea of home shifted for him: "Our home was East Lansing, Michigan. We didn't want to go back to segregation."

In East Lansing he could move freely around the campus and sometimes the outside community, because he was gaining respect and visibility as an athlete. At his football reunions, there's always a teammate or two who bring up Bubba Smith's bravado, driving around campus in a white Riviera, then leaving it in President Hannah's official parking spot, with little to no consequences beyond an occasional parking ticket. Change was coming in fits and starts in America as they navigated young adulthood and their ever-increasing popularity on campus and nationwide.

Being a Black face in a white space didn't seem to affect my dad, because he was just happy he wasn't in Texas. My dad was, and still is, a good-looking man. His strong limbs, smooth dark skin, and thousand-watt smile resulted in adoration from white girls, and likely white boys, who stared a little too long when he walked into a room. Still my dad was extremely reserved in the face of public attention. His friend Bubba Smith, also strikingly handsome, was quite possibly made for the spotlight. His physical stature and deep baritone voice, as smooth as his skin was dark, turned heads everywhere he went on campus and off.

Bubba also had a more acute sensitivity to how Black players were treated. While my dad and Bubba were becoming stars, there were other Black (and some white) players on the team who weren't on scholarship. They had to fight for playing time while juggling classes and whatever jobs they could find to pay for their tuition, housing, and meals. Bubba had a hard time holding his tongue if he felt like the coaches weren't being fair or talked down to him or other Black players.

No matter how mythological the legend of Bubba Smith would eventually become, there was more to Charles Aaron Smith than *Police Academy*, the press's obsession with his height and weight, and the cheesy decals that said, "Kill, Bubba, kill!" The truth was, for Black players at Michigan State, the philosophical ideals of Martin Luther King Jr. and John A. Hannah had never been fully executed or tested in real-world American settings. They were essentially lab rats in a well-intentioned living laboratory. Bubba tested the limits of his metaphorical cage daily.

After he passed away in 2011, I had the blessing of getting to know his college sweetheart, Marcia, who helped coordinate his memorial service. She graciously filled in so many blanks for me and was supportive of my journey to learn more about their experiences at Michigan

State. I was especially interested in Bubba's journey because I never had the chance to thank him or his father for making the introduction to Duffy Daugherty that changed my dad's life, and eventually my own. What Marcia helped me uncover was a kind and compassionate young man, who was trying to navigate the world he grew up in and the integrated spaces that were slowly opening to him and other Black men like my dad.

The *Bubba and Marcia* love story began the summer Bubba moved into an off-campus apartment with a roommate. Bubba's place was a social hub full of parties, and a parade of pretty girls on the weekends. It seemed to Marcia that everyone knew and loved Bubba, but she was a little suspicious of all the "activity" going on in the apartment below hers. Her roommate decided to invite Bubba to one of their parties, and Marcia kept her distance most of the night. When the party ended, Bubba offered to clean up.

"No, you don't have to stay," Marcia said.

"Why are you afraid of me?" he said, as he picked up trash and straightened the furniture.

"I'm not afraid of you."

"Yes, you are."

"No, I'm not. You have a parade of activity going on down there. You have a lot of *visitors*, you know."

"Oh, that's not for me, that's my roommate. Haven't you met my roommate?" he said with a smile, entertained by her mischaracterization.

Marcia was skeptical until she met Bubba's wild roommate. It was true. The excitement was all about his roommate and not Bubba. The two began to spend a lot of time together, talking about their families, campus life, and dreams. They came from very different life experiences. Marcia was white and grew up in Lansing. Bubba was Black and spent his entire life in rural, segregated Texas. They had similar values coming from Christian households, but their differences threatened to thwart the possibility that their friendship might ever turn into a romance.

After long conversations and time spent together, Bubba got up the nerve to officially ask Marcia if they could date. It caught her off guard, not because she wasn't attracted to him, but because it brought up all manner of complicated logistics. She was a smart and down-to-earth girl who wanted to be a nurse. She wasn't into football or all that came along with the attention Bubba attracted everywhere he went on campus, which made Marcia all the more endearing to him. Nevertheless, they'd both have to reconcile the ways race stood in the way of Bubba and Marcia becoming a couple.

When Bubba asked, "Can we go out?" Marcia hesitated.

This caused him to abruptly put his arm up to her face, presenting his dark skin as a smoking gun. "It's because of *this*? My skin?" he taunted.

Not to be outdone, she lifted her white arm to his and said, "It's because of *this*."

Overcome with emotion, she stepped out for some air and a good cry. She sensed in her heart that she'd grown to love him dearly. Even though she grew up in a household that didn't actively preach prejudice, Lansing was an all-white environment, so the question of dating someone Black had never come up in her experience.

She sought counsel from her pastor, who essentially asked her, "If everything else about him is compatible, does his skin color matter?"

Bubba didn't wait around for her to sort out her feelings. He may have even realized that he had complex emotions around the matter himself. He decided to go home to Texas to see his family and clear his head before the season started. On his way back to Beaumont, he dozed off behind the wheel and wrecked his car. Alone in small-town Texas, a couple hundred miles from home, he waited for his dad, Willie Ray Smith Sr., to come to his rescue.

He dialed Marcia to let her know what happened and that he was thinking of her. She was relieved that he was okay. She made Bubba's bad day a lot brighter when she told him about the conversation she had with her pastor. Marcia accepted his invitation to date and was ready and willing to deal with whatever resistance might come from her parents or anyone else in the community. Bubba was so happy that he told his parents about the girl in East Lansing who he was crazy about.

If only things were that simple for two college kids in love in 1966. Even though Bubba had guts enough to let Marcia know how he felt about her, being an actual couple wasn't going to be an easy journey. Bubba's parents warned him to be careful as he pursued a relationship with Marcia. Up in Michigan, Marcia's family was dealing with confronting their own latent prejudice and adjusting to the unknown, but Bubba's family knew exactly what could happen to a Black man who even thought about *looking* at a white woman. The South was filled with an experiential understanding that violence at the hands of white people could occur at any time—to anyone.

As a boy, early in his dad's coaching career, Bubba stumbled upon a horrific sight in Orange, Texas. A group of white men were torturing a Black man on the north side of town. Bubba quickly hid behind a bush. The men burned the letters "KKK" into the Black man's skin as he screamed. Bubba was paralyzed as the smell of burnt flesh singed horror into his being. He'd witnessed an act of hate that he wasn't able to stop. *No matter how much love you might create and experience in your own home*, he learned, *the world outside its doors is filled with hatred and violence—and there is nothing you can do about it.* Even Bubba's own mother, Georgia, suffered after she gave birth to a baby girl, who died a few days after she was born because they couldn't be seen at the white hospital, because they were Black.

I'm awed by the Smith family's resilience, and that of all Black families who suffered such traumatic events. His parents somehow managed to cultivate a strong sense of confidence in their son that was on full display by his early 20s. Instead of shrinking in the face of such horrors, he moved through the world unapologetically, taking up as much space as he possibly could. Since he'd totaled his car on the way home, he purchased a white Riviera in town and had a family friend affix gold mailbox letters spelling out B-U-B-B-A on the driver's side door. Proud to show off his new ride and get the girl, he went directly to see Marcia. He parked under her window and blasted the radio as loud as it would go. And just like that scene in *Say Anything* where John Cusack's character holds up his boom box to serenade his love, Bubba waited by the car until Marcia poked her head out of the window. She still tears up remembering how sweet and funny he looked as the song "My Girl" wafted from his car radio.

They'd overcome a major hurdle in simply deciding to give their love a shot. Navigating what that meant in practice was a whole other thing. Duffy Daugherty's Black players were popular on campus—with everyone. Especially the white girls. Yet, there was an unspoken rule that the Black players couldn't and shouldn't date them.

"He was struggling with a lot of issues being a football player at Michigan State," Marcia explained. "They weren't supposed to date white girls. They could mess around with white girls, but they weren't supposed to date them seriously."

Bubba's strategy was to essentially hide their relationship, even though slowly his teammates started to put two and two together.

"One, he didn't want somebody messing with him, telling him he couldn't spend time with me, but he also didn't want anybody messing with me for dating him." She continued, "He was pretty protective. And so it was kinda hard for us to actually date. He would go out and make the rounds—go to the places that he needed to go and be seen, and then he would come over to my apartment after and just disappear on them."

One of the few times they actually went out in public, he walked about five paces behind her, fading into the crowd while they walked home from the Lansing Theater downtown.

"What are you doing?" Marcia called to him.

"Keep going. Just keep going," he said, waving her on.

"No! I know what you're doing," she protested, stopping in the sidewalk.

He caught up to her in a few strides.

"Well, do you want people to know you're walking with a *nigger*?" he scolded.

"If I didn't want them to know I was with you, I wouldn't be with you! I'm not walking ahead of you anymore!" she fumed.

For much of the relationship they struggled with the milestones that are a normal part of falling and being in love. Bubba was reluctant to meet Marcia's parents—afraid they might reject him, or worse, physically harm him. Bubba's skittish behavior was deeply rooted in self-preservation and Marcia's protection. There was the memory of the man in north Orange, whose skin was branded by Klansmen, but also the pressure of being in the campus spotlight as a football player.

Black players who dared to date white girls *and* fall in love with them, like their teammate Ernie Pasteur, who fell in love with a girl named Micki, suffered the consequences. The general feeling was that Duffy and the other coaches didn't want any distractions drawing attention to their football program. Some in the East Lansing community had already criticized Daugherty for having too many Black players on the team. Watching MSU's Black players date white girls wasn't likely to alleviate those criticisms, so the consequences were less playing time on game day. "No interracial dating" was an unspoken rule that all the Black players knew about.

When I first encountered Ernie Pasteur and his wife, Micki, at Bubba's home the night before the memorial in 2011, I didn't know anything about the challenges they faced in their courtship. I was lost in Ernie's big smile and tales of the "Wonder Boys" and didn't even consider what they encountered as an interracial couple in the 1960s. They've been married more than 50 years, but their campus love affair was the source of both their greatest joy and a lot of pain as young people. They had a few classes together, but like Bubba and Marcia, their affection grew at a campus party. The idealism of the '60s and the climate that MSU president John A. Hannah had created in support of civil rights made dating relatively easy for Ernie and Micki. They endured stares and whatever consequences Ernie faced on the football field, but for the most part, they were able to cultivate a love connection between them that's still palpable today. They're the kind of seniors you'd cast in a pharmaceutical commercial—the way they still hold hands and post adorable pictures of their world travels on Facebook. When I'm in their presence, I feel the innermost parts of myself saying, *Everyone should be fortunate enough to know that kind of love before they die.*

Two years after Ernie and his Omega Psi Phi brothers serenaded Micki with what they called the fraternity's "Sweetheart" song, they were married at the campus church in the middle of a snowstorm. No matter how in love Micki was with the young man from Beaufort, North Carolina, her parents rejected the union and warned that they'd have trouble finding jobs, housing, and schools for their kids. Ernie's family was a bit more supportive but also feared for their future in an America that wasn't ready for their love. Their marriage was illegal in North Carolina and had only been legal in Michigan for barely one generation. As much as it hurt not to have her parents at the wedding, the most unnerving moment occurred when she and her bridesmaids, and Ernie's groomsmen—my dad, Clinton Jones, George Webster, Jim Summers, and the other Black teammates—waited for Ernie to arrive at the church during the snowstorm.

Bubba loaned Ernie his car for the day but gave him the wrong set of keys. Once they got the right key, they dug the parked car out of a few feet of snow, then made it to the church two hours late. Ernie and Micki's relationship has been filled with hard-won happily-ever-afters. Eventually Micki's parents came around and embraced Ernie a few years into their marriage. They faced discrimination throughout their union but raised healthy and successful children who made them doting grandparents.

Among the many mind-boggling things about equality in the United States is how loving a person of another ethnicity could get you arrested or murdered 50 years ago. And yet, in 2008 the country elected a biracial president and took another important step further—federal protections for same-sex marriages in 2015.

It's even a bit laughable to me how my own personal perceptions and opinions on Black and white relationships have shifted over time. When I was about five or six, my parents were close to a family called the Boones, with a white mother and a Black father. Their three honey-brown kids were fairly close in age to me and my siblings. They had two little boys, one older and one younger than me, and a teen daughter who my sisters adored. Comically, I was in the second or third grade when I realized Mrs. Boone was white.

She had long dark hair like my mom's, so in my child mind I thought she was Black. Somehow when skin color was explained to me within the context of my mother's fair olive complexion, I assumed Mrs. Boone was also just light skinned. No matter the amount of *other* ethnicities that make up my mother's DNA, she has a strong Black identity. The fact that the Boones were a family that *looked* like ours, but *wasn't* like ours, was an understanding that unfolded slowly. Until my early adulthood, it didn't occur to me that people likely perceived my mom as non-Black most of the time, in the same way that I'd misidentified Mrs. Boone as Black.

I'm not sure when I first learned the word "mixed," but it somehow came to describe the little things, like how the Boone kids' hair was sometimes a bit wild. They didn't have the epic slathering of grease and other oils laying down their soft wooly curls like we did. My sisters were getting hair relaxers in those days, and my hair was always plaited in braids or twists with plastic barrettes and gumball-sized knockers. Whereas the Boones' daughter's hair was natural and held back by a simple elastic band.

I wasn't opposed to the idea of people falling in love and getting married, no matter what color their skin was. My mother's sister
Bernice remarried after I was born. My whole life, her white husband
was simply Uncle John to me. In middle school, though, I did suffer
from an underlying low-grade irritation that, at least in Minnesota, the
framework was usually a Black man with a white woman—oftentimes
a rather plain white woman. I came into my Black womanhood surrounded by examples of smart, beautiful Black women like my older
sisters and their friends when they were in high school and college. It
seemed to me that there were a lot of beautiful, educated, and successful Black women to choose from, but that Black men saw whiteness as
a more significant measure of attractiveness than any other attribute.

We weren't exploring multicultural identity on social media back
in the '90s. Even the so-called mixed girls in our all-white community
were seen as Black by the outside world. The two or three Black boys I
remember from high school and middle school paid me and the other
Black girls no mind. Instead they dated, and a few eventually married,
white girls. My sisters had the occasional white boyfriend here and
there, and my oldest sister, Lisa, eventually married one, my brother-
in-law, Will. The white boys I went to school with seemed to have no
interest in dating me. This could have been because I was Black, and
also because I ran with a group of white kids from choir and theatre.
A few of those boys have husbands now, which also might explain why
there weren't any romantic sparks between us as teenagers.

My parents weren't too concerned about the skin color of those we
dated, as long as we were good Catholic girls. And not the stereotypical
kind. When they were in high school, my parents had study dates at
the kitchen table of my mother's home in McNair for months before
my dad finally had the courage to kiss her goodnight on the porch.
The way they tell it, and others confirm, they had a toothache-sweet
and wholesome courtship. The pretty cheerleader and the handsome
football and track star were too square to make out under the bleachers.

Funny enough, they were considered a mixed couple, not because my mother was Creole and came from a multicultural heritage, but because she was Catholic and my father was Baptist. Black people were as particular about those things back then as they are about how to prepare macaroni and cheese or potato salad for the cookout today. The idea that my mom fell for an *American* man mattered. Her family perceived themselves as *French*, even a whole 150 years after the Louisiana Purchase. Never mind that my dad's parents were also from Louisiana. The Washingtons didn't speak French and they weren't Catholic.

Luckily, my mom's parents liked my dad. They liked him so much that my grandfather Burnice would send my mom's little sister Lynette to the store for milk to go along with the steak he prepared when my dad came to visit. News of my dad's success and eventual conversion to Catholicism reached my mom's hometown by the time he asked my grandfather if he could propose to my mother. Burnice Goudeau supported my dad's proposal provided that he promised he would make sure that my mom completed her education. I've always fancied my dad a feminist in this way. I was never told that I couldn't achieve in school or life because of my gender. Knowing that my mother's father cared about her academic endeavors as much as my dad supported mine as a young woman fills my heart with gratitude.

My dad proposed during my mom's visit to East Lansing before the new school year began in 1966. My feminist bubble burst a little, though, learning that the moment was met with a lot of uncertainty for my mother. "He actually got on his knees and proposed to me. And I was shocked; I had no idea he was going to propose. I had my own plans about how I was gonna finish school and what I was gonna do. But, really being a part of his world meant that those plans were going to be dropped," she remembered.

Going into his senior year, my dad knew that being considered for the professional football draft was a possibility, but he had no sense of how that might unfold.

"I got on both knees," my dad joked about their engagement. "I wanted to make sure I put the best effort forward, you know. And I did some begging. Yeah, well, I shouldn't say begging, but persuading. I also promised her, I said, 'Look, I know your dad said that he was very concerned that you finish school, before you get married. I'll make sure that happens.'"

My mother's dream was to transfer to Berkeley and finish her degree.

"So you'll come to San Francisco after you graduate?" she asked.

"I hope I could get with the 49ers—but I don't know, Claudie," he replied, knowing his fate wasn't in his own hands.

The fact that he could promise to support her education but couldn't promise her *Berkeley* was difficult for her to accept as a young woman learning about her own agency amid the most progressive student movements in American history. She put her frustrations aside to tell her girlfriends the good news and show off her simple engagement ring.

Claudith Goudeau would have to figure out how to be a modern 20th-century woman standing on her own two feet *and* become Mrs. Gene Washington. She excitedly accepted the challenge, but a few haters at the junior college laughed in her face when word got around.

"You're not engaged to Gene Washington," a girl remarked.

"Yes, I am!" my mom fumed.

"Gene Washington is engaged to *Cynthia*," another girl said, sucking her teeth.

Flummoxed and concerned, my mom dialed up my dad in East Lansing and demanded an explanation for this cruelty.

He laughed and explained, "There's another Gene Washington who plays football, Clau. He goes to Stanford."

This put my mother at ease, knowing their engagement was still very much on, but it didn't resolve her fears about whether or not marriage would interrupt her ability to finish her education at Berkeley.

CHAPTER
THIRTEEN

Mid-November 1966 brought a biting chill to the campus air, the kind that occurs in the Midwest after Halloween when fall transitions into something resembling a slight weather tantrum just before Thanksgiving. The week of November 13, in particular, the weather flaunted lows in the teens and highs in the 50s. I imagine the wind duked it out with the last of the autumn leaves desperately clinging to their branches as winter aggressively advanced on the Red Cedar River.

It may have been nostalgia or all the news clippings accumulated over Eugene Washington's college years that prompted some community members in La Porte to raise funds so that my grandfather could attend my dad's final game in Spartan Stadium against Notre Dame. Imagine Henry Washington, on a plane for the first time, heading to a brutally cold East Lansing, Michigan, to see my dad play football.

As my dad told it, "I was more excited about Dad coming than I was about the game, because Dad had never seen me play college football in a live situation. As a matter of fact, he never saw me play football even in high school."

It occurred to me when I probed further just how removed my grandfather was from my dad's incredible football life at the time. He wasn't into sports and only allowed my dad to participate when some men in the community invited him to join their baseball league. My dad's coaches brought him home from practice throughout his baseball, basketball, track, and football seasons. To this day, I still don't understand why his dad wasn't more present in his life in support of his athletic achievements. My grandfather was a dependable provider, a deacon in the church, and built a small business on their property where local teens could hang out. Still, I wondered how it made my dad feel to excel in something that his entire hometown, Black and white, was praising him for, but to not have his father in the stands rooting for him.

I wanted to ask, but when I opened my mouth, all that came out was, "He never saw you play?"

"He was very supportive, but he was really not into college sports or even high school sports. So with him coming and seeing the game? It meant a lot. That was my last college game. With the people in La Porte supporting—a lot of the businesspeople supporting, I was very proud," he said with a smile.

I can only imagine what it meant for both of them to be in one another's presence in this way. During so much of my dad's experience at Michigan State, he was alone and without the physical presence and support of his family. He didn't go home for holidays or summer breaks. The idea that my grandfather was willing to take such a journey, as a Black man who'd only known Jim Crow, says a lot about his love and desire to support my dad. Even if it came late in his college career.

My relationship with my dad was similar in a way. He didn't know the first thing about a pirouette or acting in a dramatic scene on stage. My choir teacher in high school was a devotee of sacred choral music, performed in a very classical and Caucasian manner, which had a lulling effect on my dad after a long day at work. If I caught a glimpse of him in the audience from the stage, he was usually dozing off during the dry-as-toast concerts. It made me laugh inside, but it also stung a little. Both of my parents supported my involvement in the arts, but my dad fell asleep during the performances, and my mom would cuss me out about having to pay for something related to the performance on the car ride home.

Still, they were there. In the stands, in the audience, at the banquets, and wherever else they were dutifully committed to be for my sisters and me. My sisters' children are now teenagers, and I get to play the role of devoted auntie at their school activities. It's as if I have a tiny glimpse into what it must have been like for my hardworking parents to keep up with our events when we were young. I realize how precious it is that, whether my dad was awake for every performance or not, he was there. He might not have understood every detail or the technique behind the work, but he appreciated the arts and my development as an artist. When my mom was still trying to persuade me to be a doctor my senior year in high school, my dad was calling up the admissions office at Juilliard to see if they'd selected their freshman BFA acting cohort. I got the exciting and disappointing news that I was wait-listed as the first female alternate for the acting program from my dad, weeks before I received the formal letter in the mail.

My dad took time out of his 3M recruiting trip to Southern California to see me perform the role of Juanita in James Baldwin's *Blues for Mister Charlie*, after I'd passionately petitioned the USC theatre school to select main stage productions that better represented the African American students in the program. My little activism shifted things in the department, and students today have opportunities that students of color didn't when I was there. The more I learn about my dad's college years, I realize that my choosing the arts rather than connecting with him through sports might have made it challenging for us to share a common interest. We can't get those years back, or play the *what if I'd embraced sports instead of trying so hard not to be in Gene Washington's shadow?* game. The truth is, when I think about the most significant moments in my arts career, my dad was always there.

When my grandfather arrived on the MSU campus in 1966, the energy in East Lansing was alight with anticipation as game day

approached. After the prior year's defeat in the Rose Bowl, a final stand
with Notre Dame was the last hope for the Spartans in defending their
Big Ten and National Champion titles. In the 1960s, the Rose Bowl had
a "no repeat" rule for teams. This meant that since the Spartans played
in the 1966 Rose Bowl, despite the fact that they were undefeated and
ranked number one in the Big Ten during my dad's senior year, they
couldn't return to Pasadena. Back then there wasn't the abundance of
post-season "Bowl" games named after fruit, snacks, fast food, or video
game consoles that we have today. This final showdown with Notre
Dame was their one and only shot at ending their season on top.

The stakes were high and everyone was *fired up and ready to go*,
as my dad likes to say. There were pep rallies, intense practices, and
reports of professors canceling classes in anticipation of the game. The
media ran with the excitement of the number-one and number-two
ranked teams going head to head in what they coined the "Game of the
Decade." The game was initially set for regional broadcast by ABC. The
network received so many letters from frustrated fans around the country, and even a few inmates who followed football, that ABC eventually
agreed to air the game on delay nationally.

Coming off an undefeated season, the Spartans dominated to such
a degree that being ranked number two could only be explained by the
close game they'd played weeks earlier against Ohio State, on October
15, 1966. Since the game was so close, and Notre Dame crushed North
Carolina's Tar Heels 32–0 on the exact same day, they held the number-one spot moving forward. Spartan fans felt the only reason MSU
wasn't ranked number one was because they'd beaten Ohio State 11–8, a
slim margin of only three points. The pollsters didn't take into account
that the game was played in a downpour, making it impossible to see
from one side of the field to the other.

Duffy's opinion was that since the Spartans dominated in the first
half, then fought back during terrible conditions in the fourth quarter,
driving 80 yards for the winning touchdown, the polls should have

considered more than only the final score against Ohio State when determining the ranking going into the matchup against Notre Dame.

Duffy believed in good sportsmanship and "common decency." In his memoir he explained why he didn't believe in embarrassing another team to influence the polls:

> The Irish had a tough time against Purdue, but the week after our Ohio State victory we manhandled Purdue. We were leading 28-0 and could have made it 60-0, but we used our reserves throughout the second half and wound up winning 41-20. I never believed in running up the score just to impress some pollsters.

Devout Catholics or not, Notre Dame had no problem running up the scoreboard something terrible. They wreaked havoc on every team on their schedule, including Duke 64–0 the week before, as if it were the Crusades. Perusing the final scores on their 1966 schedule, it seems to me that Notre Dame's head coach, Ara Parseghian, wasn't concerned with controlling the scoreboard but crushing it. The tension around the rankings made for great media fodder and further excited fans on both sides. Michigan State played nine games that season, whereas Notre Dame had only eight, with one left to go the following week against USC. Even though the Irish had played fewer games, they won the favor of the polls. The team was ranked number one going into game day on November 19, 1966.

I doubt my grandfather cared much about polls, but I imagine the hoopla surrounding the game let him know that it was pretty significant. The Spartans had a lot to prove and resigned themselves to settling the poll controversy on the field. Team practice sessions increased in intensity as the week progressed. The defense dissected every inch of Notre Dame film they could get their hands on. Coaches Hank Bullough and Vince Carillot focused heavily on preparing the defense for the Fighting Irish passing game. They centered their attention on Terry Hanratty, the Notre Dame quarterback, and wide receiver Jim Seymour's patterns. As they fixed their eyes on the film projections of Hanratty and Seymour and plotted each Spartan player's assignment, unbridled testosterone filled the room. They were literally ready to take Notre Dame's high-scoring heads off by Friday evening.

While my dad focused on pass patterns in preparation for the big game, his teammates found themselves caught up in the media swarm. News cameras from CBS followed Jimmy Raye and Bubba around campus earlier in the week. In the footage, they look as docile as the Hardy Boys from the popular 1960s mystery novels, walking to and from classes. You would never know they were preparing for the dogfight of their lives. In one clip that I found online, they walk down a campus sidewalk in their practice jerseys and sweatpants. The giant Bubba Smith looks like an old-school Bruce Wayne to Jimmy Raye's Boy Wonder. They are the spitting image of two superheroes preparing for the most significant game of their college careers, but the news segment makes them look like they are discussing how much mayonnaise the other prefers on his turkey sandwich and not the heap of hurt they wish to put on Notre Dame.

When the cameras weren't around, Bubba invited Jimmy on a joyride to blow off some steam before their team meeting Friday afternoon. They weren't due at the Kellogg Center, where the team stayed the night before games, until 6:00 p.m. Bubba thought it would make for a good time to take a little spin around campus.

Bubba picked Jimmy up from Wilson Hall and they traveled across campus to Hagadorn Road and proceeded to Grand River Avenue in his Bubba-mobile, the mailbox letters B-U-B-B-A affixed to the driver's side door, right under the window.

"We start up Grand River and the street was full of people. You know everybody is in town for the game, and there is only one guy with a big white car with a sunroof in the whole state of Michigan. Bubba.

We were rolling up Grand River—we had to go slow because there were so many people in the streets. Bubba is high-fiving and waving at everybody. We're enjoying the ride! We get to the corner of Abbott Road and Grand River and a police car pulls up behind us," Jimmy said with a laugh.

This is where their personal accounts of what happened next diverge. According to Bubba's memoir, *Kill, Bubba, Kill!*, when the two were pulled over, the officer announced that Bubba had $1,500 in traffic tickets and that there was a warrant for his arrest. Bubba was handcuffed and thrown in a cell with inmates who recognized him as an MSU football player. Bubba told Jimmy to call Duffy while he sat in the cell talking football with his new jail mates. Around the two-hour mark, athletic director Biggie Munn arrived at the jailhouse to bail him out and threatened the police chief, saying, "Do you like your job?" Biggie then secured Bubba's release.

In Jimmy's version, after they were pulled over, the officer requested that they follow him to the East Lansing police station, where Bubba was arrested for outstanding parking tickets totaling *$5,000*.

As Jimmy continued with his side of the story, I slid to the front of my chair, awaiting the 50-year-old tea to be solidly spilled.

"Bubb said, 'Call Duffy.' And then he said, 'No, call Biggie.' And so I call Biggie Munn and tell him we were in the East Lansing police station. He said, 'What are you doing over there?' Then I said, 'Yeah, Bubba got stopped for some parking tickets.' So he asked to speak to the chief of police or whatever. The chief of police of East Lansing got on the phone and he and Biggie talked, and I guess they said, 'Just let him go,' or whatever, and we were able to leave and then get to Kellogg Center," he recounted, barely able to hold back his laughter.

When they finally arrived at Kellogg Center for their team dinner and meeting, it appeared that no one noticed that anything was out of the ordinary. Defensive coaches Hank Bullough and Vince Carillot both told me they didn't know anything about the incident. I've had a chance to sit down with both coaches over the past few years, and the fact that both Coach Bullough and Coach Carillot gave me puzzled looks when I asked them about the joyride still tickles me to no end. I can only conclude that Duffy and Biggie Munn were able to keep the rest of the football staff in the dark about Bubba and Jimmy's adventure and focus on the game.

A few miles away, the Fighting Irish were facing a little excitement of their own after a two-hour train ride from South Bend. As the train carrying the team into town for the game settled on the tracks, Notre Dame fans greeted them on the platform with "Go Irish" signs and excited cheers. The team proudly filed out of the passenger car and onto the icy platform. In a September 1986 interview with Sam Smith of the *Chicago Tribune*, All-American running back Nick Eddy recounted the precise moment that things took a grim turn: "I had on a new pair of wing tips that night and it was cold and damp . . . I slipped on the metal steps and when I lost my balance, I grabbed a hold of something and pulled the shoulder again."

Nick had partially dislocated his shoulder after he was tackled in Notre Dame's game against Pittsburgh two weeks earlier. He'd nursed the injury and was able to play in a game against Duke the previous week, but the mishap on the train platform took Nick Eddy out of the lineup for Saturday morning. Despite the fact that the day was filled with more than a little excitement, both teams were certain that November 19, 1966, would bring them a win when their heads hit their pillows Friday night.

Over 80,000 people arrived on campus the following morning and began to fill Spartan Stadium by noon. My grandfather Henry Washington took his seat, surrounded by thousands of white fans cheering his son and the Spartan team as they emerged from the tunnel, miles away from Jim Crow for the first time in his life. Clinton Jones described the moment as preparing for war. Defeat was not an option.

They wanted to prove to everyone around the country that they were indeed the best.

ABC TV opened the coverage, calling it the "Game of the Decade," as the pregame rituals of college football unfolded on delay across 48 states, and for the first time for US troops stationed in Vietnam, and in Hawaii, home of running back Bob Apisa and kicker Dick Kenney. As ABC covered the game from multiple angles, including close-ups of the players on the field, it was glaring how different the Spartans looked demographically from Notre Dame's nearly all-white team.

This "Game of the Decade" would prove to be a major milestone in American race relations. Whether they knew it or not, the teams were playing for more than just a National Championship. MSU's team, with 20 Black players and 11 Black starters, had been called the "Grambling of the North." The racists poked fun at how Black Daugherty's team was, at the same time that Black fans and Pacific Islanders across the country applauded. Symbolically, this epic match between Notre Dame, with only one Black player, Alan Page, and the Spartans, whose starting lineup was Blacker than any seen at a predominantly white institution *ever*, signaled a turning point in college football history. This was the first time a college football team looked like the demographics we see on the field today.

The years leading to this moment were brutal and bloody for Black Americans attempting to exercise their full freedoms under the protection of new laws. Without much physical sanctuary from violent forms of racism resisting the new legislation, progress was slow. Those with any economic or political power did everything and anything to uphold white supremacy because federal laws had made their way of life illegal seemingly overnight. The backlash that Black communities received in response to their audacity to assert their rights to full citizenship under the law—the right to vote, the right to worship, access to quality education, the use of public restrooms and facilities, and other basic rights Americans today take for granted—yielded more murders, physical abuse, harassment, and economic discrimination.

A month earlier, on October 15, 1966 (the same day my dad and his Spartan teammates were fighting for their win against Ohio State in a downpour), Huey P. Newton and Bobby Seale formed the Black Panther Party in Oakland, California. The second half of 1966 was increasingly about an assertion of *Black Power* as a slogan of Black empowerment in the face of white supremacy and oppression. This final game at Notre Dame was an opportunity to show everyone around the country, on broadcast television, that this fully integrated Spartan team could be National Champions for a second year in a row under the leadership of its Black quarterback, Jimmy Raye, and Black team captains George "Mickey" Webster and Clinton Jones. As they stepped onto the field, they concerned themselves only with the goal of securing a win for MSU, not realizing the impact that this physical embodiment of integration before 33 million viewers and 80,000 fans would have on future generations.

Notre Dame won the toss, but the luck of the Fighting Irish quickly ran out during the first quarter. As if Nick Eddy slipping on the train platform Friday night wasn't enough, the Spartan defense delivered on hours of preparation with Hanratty and Seymour as their primary targets. Bubba Smith, Charlie "Mad Dog" Thornhill, George Webster, Jess Phillips, and the Spartan defense were ready, willing, and dead set on showing their ability to anticipate every move of Hanratty's offense.

The game was hard-hitting gridiron football. In the first quarter, Bubba plowed into Notre Dame quarterback Terry Hanratty so hard that it caused a shoulder separation. The primary target of the Spartan defense was completely knocked out of the game, thanks to big Bubba, number 95. Notre Dame coach Ara Parseghian replaced Hanratty with Coley O'Brien, who had been diagnosed with diabetes weeks earlier. The Spartan defense had put all of their energy toward shutting down Hanratty, not O'Brien, during their game preparation. Coley O'Brien hadn't even been on their radar in the weeks leading up to the game. The replacement brought a different rhythm than they'd anticipated. The Spartans had to adjust their focus with every scoring attempt and effort to shut down the Irish offense. Two plays after Hanratty's shoulder separation, the "Kill, Bubba, kill!" chanting coming from the stands continued to manifest on the field when another one of Bubba's casualties, Notre Dame center George Goeddeke, a Detroit native, sprained his ankle covering a punt.

These were 19- and 20-something-year-old kids on the field fighting for the win like strays in a dogfight. I can only imagine the horror my grandfather must have felt seeing Bubba Smith from Beaumont, Texas, take out Notre Dame's white offense one by one. Seeing players helped off the field after an intense hit is cringeworthy for most people, but especially for a parent with a child on that same field. In a stadium filled with white spectators, he must have held his breath with the crowd roaring every time Jimmy Raye threw long to his son, Eugene. Then exhaled when my dad's hands made contact with the ball only long enough to wince when the Irish defense brought my dad to his knees moments after.

As the Irish attempted to shuffle their roster to replace the three star players who were now on the bench (Nick Eddy, Terry Hanratty, and George Goeddeke), the Spartans scored on Notre Dame like few other teams had done that entire season. By the second quarter, Michigan State finally scored after a touchdown by Regis Cavender. Instantly the Spartans became the first team to score on the Irish all season. The Spartan defense held strong, ensuring that the Irish wouldn't have room to run up the score the way they'd become accustomed to slaughtering other teams all season.

The game continued to favor the Spartans when Dick Kenney kicked a 47-yard field goal with his bare foot. The Spartans were up 10–0, and everything Daugherty and his team had worked so hard for was unfolding with great momentum. The cheerleaders jumped with giddiness. Long white streamers littered the sidelines as if someone had thrown toilet paper rolls from the stands. The drama and intrigue persisted as the Spartans responded to the relatively unknown Notre Dame backup quarterback, Coley O'Brien. Although there are claims that he was given candy bars, orange juice, and insulin on the sidelines to manage his diabetes throughout, O'Brien was able to get around the Spartan defense when he launched a 34-yard touchdown to Bob Gladieux.

In the second half, the ABC cameras opened on a shot of the MSU smokestack in the distance from a high angle of the crowd. A cloud of gray smoke wafted upward from the mouth of the stack, where a Notre Dame player hanged in effigy from its rim, serving as a reminder of the days when America didn't cringe at the sight or even the symbolism of lynching. The Michigan State offense and defense pressed hard, and the Fighting Irish fought back with scores throughout the second half. Coley O'Brien weathered hit after hit, and helped the Irish rush for 70 yards, ending with Joe Azzaro's 28-yard kick into the uprights. The kick brought the score to a 10–10 tie. With Hanratty long out of the game, the last of the Spartans' targets, Jim Seymour, was effectively shut down by the Spartans' defense, who'd studied and successfully blocked the Irish passing game before the wide receiver could even get his hands on the ball.

In the fourth quarter, Jimmy Raye threw a pass that was intercepted by Notre Dame safety Tom Schoen, setting off a gasp-inducing series. Just when it seemed that Schoen had decisively turned the tables, Phil Hoag and Bubba Smith hit the Irish halfback, Dave Haley, for an eight-yard loss on the second play. On the third-down pass, Coley O'Brien didn't make contact with his receiver. When they went for the 41-yard field goal kick by Joe Azzaro, the crowd watched the ball sail through the air, then veer too far right of the goal post.

With only a minute and a half to go, Notre Dame coach Ara Parseghian played it safe by running the ball up the middle rather than risk a turnover. With every play, the Spartan defense and the crowd grew impatient. "Why aren't you trying to win?" they protested, looking to their coaches on the sideline and throwing up their hands in frustration.

The seconds on the scoreboard clock ticked down to zero, and the "Game of the Decade" accepted its place in history as the "Game of the Century," ending in a 10–10 tie. The overhead angle from ABC is possibly the most anticlimactic end-of-game moment I've ever seen. A faint rumble of boos and groans underscored the moment. Immediately following the game and for years to come, Michigan State players were frustrated that Parseghian chose to run out the clock and not play for the win. Notre Dame's coach defended this choice, understanding that they'd have a good chance against USC the following week. Risking a turnover was not in their best interest. Parseghian's decision has continued to receive criticism over 50 years later.

The College Football Researchers Association named the Spartans National Champions, while the Helms Athletic Foundation and the National Football Foundation named them Co-National Champions, and the two teams shared the MacArthur trophy. Now that I actually understand how disappointing their Rose Bowl defeat was, it really hits me that my dad's college career ended without the satisfaction of an outright claim to the National Champion title.

When my grandfather returned to La Porte on Sunday, I'm sure he had to tell the story of the tie when neighbors stopped by well into the new year. It was an intense and fascinating game. Watching it all these years later, I can still feel the grit of the players on both sides and their collective will to win. It makes sports journalists' lists as one of the top games of college football history year after year. Historians argue that the MSU versus Notre Dame game of 1966 is still of interest to sports enthusiasts over 50 years later mainly because it ended in a tie. Perhaps, in time, we'll also grow to consider and acknowledge the impact the game had on race relations, or at least the ways that it opened up the argument that full racial integration of the sport could, and would, be key to winning national championships.

In 2016, a gathering of members from the Notre Dame and Michigan State 1966 football teams occurred in East Lansing, Michigan. On both sides, with the distance of 50 years, the men recognized they were part of a historic event that had a lasting impact on their lives and the country. My dad's teammate Pat Gallinagh enjoys giving people a trivia challenge as a means of highlighting just how significant the game was.

Gallinagh asks with a glint in his eye, "Who were the 1976 National Champions? The 1986 champs? How about 1996 or 2006?"

Most people (including me) have no clue what the answers to those questions are. Die-hard college football fans know who the National Champions were in 1966 because of the 10–10 tie. Maybe I didn't know that my dad's team was such a significant part of college football history for most of my life, but proudly I know it now. I know that every yard gained, and every play stopped, had an impact on what was possible for my dad's ability to create a better life for himself and his new fiancée, my mom.

God of our weary years
God of our silent tears

Thou who has brought us
thus far on the way

Thou who has by Thy might
led us into the light

Keep us forever in the path,
we pray.

———

From the Black National Anthem,
"Lift Every Voice and Sing," by James Weldon Johnson

CHAPTER

FOURTEEN

He was in between classes when the MSU Athletics Department tracked him down to say he had a phone call. When my dad got to the football office, he picked up the phone and a man on the other end said, "Congratulations, Gene, you have been drafted in the first round by the Minnesota Vikings. We're so happy and excited that you will be joining us—and by the way, Bud Grant will be our new coach, and he is coming down from Winnipeg."

My dad interrupted him. "Well, sir, may I ask who I'm speaking to?"

The voice on the other end of the phone said, "I'm Sid Hartman. And I'm a reporter for the *Minneapolis Star Tribune.*"

About a week later, the Vikings called him.

My mother was the first person he told that he'd be going to the NFL. It was early March, 1967, and their wedding was set for June in San Francisco.

"Minnesota?" She gasped. "What happened to San Francisco?"

She'd hoped my dad would go to the 49ers, so Minnesota had never crossed her mind. At the school library she looked at a map to figure out where exactly *Minnesota* was. Her plans to attend Berkeley slipped away after one phone call. As if life wanted to mock her further, the *other* Gene Washington at Stanford, also a wide receiver, who was betrothed to that girl named Cynthia, was drafted by the 49ers two years later, in 1969.

My mother's adventure in California would come to an end after their wedding, and she'd start a new life in Minnesota as a married woman. The overall good fortune of my dad being drafted in the first round, as the number-eight pick, was greater than her disappointment around where they'd reside. They were so focused on getting my dad through his senior year and what the next chapter would bring that the fact that my dad was part of NFL Draft history was lost on them at the time. For the first and only time in professional football history, four players from the same college team, all African American, were drafted in the first round, within the first eight picks.

Bubba Smith, the man who made it possible for my dad to receive a scholarship to Michigan State, was the number-one pick overall and drafted by the Baltimore Colts. The number-two spot went to my dad's Bobbsey Twin, Clinton Jones, who was the number-one pick for the Minnesota Vikings. George "Mickey" Webster was selected fifth overall by the Houston Oilers, and my dad solidified the historic moment as the eighth pick overall and second pick to the Minnesota Vikings. Michigan State's contribution to ethnic diversity in the pros continued when three additional teammates, also African American, were drafted. Jeff Richardson went to the New York Jets in the sixth round. Jim Summers went to the Denver Broncos, and Charlie "Mad Dog" Thornhill was drafted to the Boston Patriots in the ninth round. Their kicker from Hawaii, Dick Kenney, was drafted by the Philadelphia Eagles in the 14th round.

In 1967, the draft was a far cry from the spectacle it's become today. The official draft itself occurred in New York from March 14 to March 15, 1967. But the Vikings general manager, Jim Finks, was in the hospital recovering from a gallbladder surgery, so instead of joining the other teams and their leadership in New York, the Vikings completed their draft choices from Finks's hospital room in Minnesota. After securing my dad as the second pick for the team after his MSU teammate Clinton Jones, the Vikings were given the 15th pick overall. They used their pick to select Notre Dame's Alan Page, the only Black player on the field for the Fighting Irish months earlier in the "Game of the Century" that ended in a 10–10 tie.

Much like the politics of the country at the time, professional football in the United States was in the process of a major transition, and race was only part of that. Prior to 1967, pro football was played under two leagues: the American Football League (AFL) and the National Football League (NFL). In June 1966, the two entities settled on a four-year plan to become one organization, which we now know as the NFL. Before the merger, the NFL and AFL competed for the best new talent during their respective annual drafts. The AFL's strong economic power allowed for intense bidding wars between the leagues for signing players, driving up the asking price for a draft pick that resulted in high six-figure salaries. With this competition eliminated by the merger of the two leagues and a common draft, my dad and others drafted in 1967 didn't see the same starting salaries as their predecessors selected in the first round before the merger. The average NFL salary in 1966 was dramatically lower, at approximately $23,600 per year.

In a parallel universe, professional basketball was in the process of similar changes. The American Basketball Association (ABA) surfaced in 1967 as a challenger to the National Basketball Association (NBA). Primarily based on their high school basketball records, my dad and Bubba Smith both were drafted to professional basketball teams weeks after the 1967 football draft. My dad was selected by the ABA's Indiana Pacers in the 12th round as their last selection for the year. Bubba was the 114th pick in the 11th round by the NBA's Baltimore Bullets. My dad's love of basketball, and recreational pickup games on the MSU campus with Bubba and George "Mickey" Webster between football and track practices, might have led him to accept a spot on the

Pacers roster, had he not accepted his opportunity with the NFL. As he remembers it, he found out he was drafted to professional basketball from an announcement in a newspaper. No one from the Pacers actually contacted him, so it became more of a random footnote in his athletic history and not a concrete opportunity he considered pursuing.

He also had one more championship to grab in the spring of 1967. Even though the football season was over, he was still an NCAA athlete with a Big Ten outdoor track meet ahead of him. His last and final opportunity to defend his 1966 title in the 120-yard high hurdles ended with a record-setting time of 13.7 seconds that stands to this day.

Spending the past few years in the annals of my dad's MSU history has given me a better appreciation for all of the trophies and awards adorning the walls of his man cave. The room where I spent hours playing Barbie Dolls or typing up high school papers on the family computer has come alive for me in all of the medals and titles won, championship rings, accolades, and news clippings chronicling a history that's always been just under my nose.

My dad earned more medals, trophies, designations, and championships in his four years at Michigan State than I could ever conceive of acquiring in my entire lifetime. By the time he was ready to sign his Minnesota Vikings contract at the end of his college athletics career, my dad had achieved Academic All-America, All-Big Ten, and All-America. He was an NCAA, Big Ten, and Central Collegiate Champion in both indoor and outdoor track from 1965 to 1966, only slowing down his senior year to achieve the one last Outdoor Big Ten Champion title in 1967 in the 120-yard high hurdles. He was named Athlete of the Year for 1964 to 1965 and received the Big Ten Conference Medal of Honor in 1967. He was also recognized as a Michigan State University Outstanding Senior. He was honored by Sparta Athletic and Excalibur Senior Men's Honorary for his academic achievements that same year.

In hindsight, if I'd known how incredible he was as both a student and an athlete, I might have been even more intimidated by his and my mother's achievements than I already was as a teenager and young adult. It has finally settled in my bones just how hard he worked and how significantly that hard work was affirmed. I amassed a few marble and gold-painted trophies throughout my dance years, but the level of achievement my dad accomplished at Michigan State is something only athletes or the truest of fans can fully appreciate. Given that he came from a segregated community, where they received hand-me-down books and occasionally athletic equipment, with no formal recognition from the mainstream newspapers for competing in *Colored* leagues, it's truly incredible that my dad was given an opportunity to meet his full athletic and academic potential at Michigan State University.

My dad and men of his generation from La Porte, Baytown, and Beaumont speak of how many talented Black athletes lived in their communities. No matter how much of that athletic talent and academic potential was cultivated in southern states in the 1950s and 1960s, white supremacy and racism kept those young men (and women, prior to Title IX) from full participation in higher education as athletes or even as students. It was grace that allowed my dad's passion for sports to cross paths with Bubba Smith and his father, Willie Ray Smith Sr. That grace extended throughout the Vietnam draft, which disproportionately impacted Black communities and other working-class ethnic groups who couldn't afford college, one of few deferment avenues available to draft-eligible young men. Not only were they able to leave a segregated environment, they also happened to be enrolled at Michigan State, contributing significantly to their football team from 1964 to 1966—key years for increased US involvement in Vietnam.

La Porte and Baytown, Texas, my parents' hometowns, had a total of 17 casualties during Vietnam. Bubba's hometown of Beaumont, Texas, had 29. While Bubba had opportunities to consider other northern schools, Michigan State was my dad's sole option. It's sobering to think about how luck and talent meeting opportunity set my dad on a course that literally changed his fate. He was never drafted in the war that killed over 58,000 US service members and millions of North and South Vietnamese military and civilians on both sides. My dad and his teammates at Michigan State were part of a social destiny that can't be fully appreciated without the distance of 50 years. Their success paved the way for the full integration of college football at the same time the United States and parts of the world were seemingly falling apart.

I've always perceived football as a violent and brutal sport. However, the action the Spartans saw on the field was nothing compared to the battles fought on the ground in North and South Vietnam, or in the streets of Watts, Selma, Montgomery, Chicago, Cleveland, and San Francisco. Yet, for whatever reason, Americans of all backgrounds love football. Some whites in the Lansing community and parts of Detroit weren't ready to live next door to a Black person or have their kids attend the same school, but they had just enough dissonance to embrace the Spartan football team and the Black men on it.

For Black people living anywhere the games were broadcast, my dad and his teammates became a symbol of what was possible for Black athletes. It was almost a foreshadowing of the Black liberation in America to come, in gains that occurred one yard at a time. They had a physical agency on the field that most Black men didn't experience in their day-to-day interactions with white people. If Bubba Smith were to stomp around Beaumont, Texas, like Godzilla, separating white boys' shoulders for the mere sport of it, he wouldn't have made it to his 22nd birthday. On the football field, this behavior was both tolerated and applauded, accompanied by the thundering whooping of "Kill, Bubba, kill!" from the stands. Football created a microcosm where the rules of race in America were suspended for four quarters. For in this little hollow of American life, they were free to "Fight for the only colors, Green and White," as their fight song boasted, suspending the *Black versus white* binary that held them, and even the Hawaiians on the team, captive.

For everyone, the Spartans of the 1960s were a welcome distraction from the nightly news and morning papers littered with war, civil rights, and labor protests. For a few hours on any given autumn Saturday, Americans in the Midwest could tuck away the letters from their sons and daughters overseas—which served as constant reminders that one's loyalty and patriotic responsibility were subjective and precarious—and enjoy a good old American football game.

Their athletic ability and the favor they'd won with fans all over the country allowed their services as football players to become commodities as my dad, Bubba Smith, Clinton Jones, and George "Mickey" Webster signed their first contracts. My dad was focused on his final months of eligibility on the MSU track team and postponed the completion of his contract to June. He looked for support from back home in La Porte, rather than sign with a big city sports agent or lawyer. He put his faith and trust in a prominent real estate family under the guidance of its patriarch, Frank Boyle Sr., to help him with his contract and financial management. The Vikings made him an offer of $150,000, to be spread out over five years. This meant about $25,000 was his annual salary, and the rest was a bonus. He accepted what he was offered.

With the guidance of Mr. Boyle, my dad slowly acquired commercial buildings that he rented out to merchant businesses, and also acquired some land in La Porte, Texas. We have no way of knowing for sure, but it's possible that no other Black man in La Porte had ever owned that much commercial real estate, and most in the community didn't realize my dad was the owner because much of the day-to-day management was handled by the Boyle family. With an investment plan in place and the first of his NFL funds in his pocket, he was able to give my mother a small budget to plan their wedding a week later.

My mother bought a wedding dress at JCPenney and helped her family book flights to San Francisco. Most of my dad's friends were in East Lansing and Detroit, preparing for his MSU teammate and new Vikings brother Clinton Jones's wedding to Laverne Key, who'd selected

the exact same wedding date, June 17, 1967. My mother had no problem enlisting bridesmaids and groomsmen from her numerous family
members and Bay Area friends, since my dad's Michigan State family
would be at Clinton and Laverne's nuptials.

My mom chose satiny Army green gowns with matching hats for
the women and stunning gray pinstriped suits with cravat ties for the
men. When my dad arrived in San Francisco, he found a jeweler to pick
out rings and stopped into a travel agency. He sat down in the office,
perused a few brochures, and booked a trip to Hawaii for their honeymoon. Family members flew in from their hometowns of Baytown and
La Porte, a first plane ride for many of them. My mother's father was
in poor health and unable to fly so my grandmother's brother, Gilbert
Williams, stood in to walk my mother down the aisle. They were married in a beautiful Catholic Mass followed by a reception at the local
Longshoremen's Hall.

Old family movies from the wedding and Hawaiian honeymoon
carve out images of a young and beautiful well-dressed couple like
the teenyboppers in all the *Beach Blanket* movies of the 1960s. They
took turns behind the Super 8 camera—my dad's dark skin as warm
as Sidney Poitier's, walking in front of a tourist site, then a quick cut
to my mother grinning from ear to ear in a canopy dress, looking like
Lena Horne's twin sister. They were the stuff that *Jet* and *Ebony* magazines were made of, never mind the fact that they were two country
kids exploring a world my grandparents could never have imagined.
The grainy vegetation and my mother's elegant poses in front of the
postmodern architecture make it hard to imagine that miles away, what
would later be called the Long, Hot Summer of 1967 was unfolding on
the mainland.

Across the country, the weight of an unpopular war and racial and
economic discrimination gave way to riots and clashes between Black
civilians and mostly white police forces nationwide. From April to May
1967, incidents occurred in Omaha, Nebraska; Nashville, Tennessee;

Louisville, Kentucky; Cleveland and Massillon, Ohio; Wichita, Kansas; Jackson, Mississippi; San Francisco, Vallejo, and San Diego, California; Houston, Texas; and Chicago, Illinois. In June, while my dad was signing his contract and my mom was selecting wedding flowers, violence erupted in Boston, Massachusetts; Clearwater and Tampa, Florida; Prattville, Alabama; Cincinnati, Ohio; Los Angeles, California; Philadelphia, Pennsylvania; Montgomery, Alabama; Maywood, Illinois; and Dayton and Middletown, Ohio.

On June 15, 1967, the *Lansing State Journal* in Michigan reported on a three-and-a-half-hour confrontation between "Negro youths and police on the west side." According to the newspaper, police dispersed a crowd of 100 to 150 youth demonstrators, some as young as five years old. Only one person was arrested for being disorderly and another for battling with police. Property damage and a few injuries were reported. On June 16, 1967, the headline read "Negro Unrest Erupts Once More in Two-Block Area of West Side" after Black teens threw rocks and bottles at cars and damaged street signs on the eve of my parents' wedding day. The white police chief, Derold W. Husby, interviewed the community as rocks were thrown from behind houses and bushes. The Black families he spoke to lamented that they were having trouble getting housing and insurance coverage. My parents took their vows on June 17 in San Francisco, as five people were arraigned on charges related to the weekend events in Lansing. By the time my parents made it to Minnesota to look for a new home, skin tinted by the Hawaiian coastline's fun and sun, the fire of discontent spread to Buffalo, New York, and Roanoke, Virginia, the hometown of my dad's MSU teammate Charlie "Mad Dog" Thornhill.

In the North, South, East, West, and midwestern spaces in between, Black youth were losing their patience. Black people faced discrimination in housing, jobs, and education—nearly every aspect of the American dream that capitalism promises. Their white counterparts, disillusioned by consumerism and a war that was killing them, too, took their protests to the streets and grew out their hair as long as their distrust of the US government. Youth were pitted against their parents and the militarized law enforcement agencies tasked with controlling them. Americans of all ethnic backgrounds were dying in Vietnam and on the streets of major cities for the promise of democracy. The tired, the poor, and the huddled masses yearning to breathe free reacted out of frustration to the policies binding them. The Chicano movement, the Asian American movement, the feminist movement, the American Indian Movement, the disability rights movement, and the gay rights movement to come were inextricably linked to the ideological cauldron churning in the belly of America's urban centers.

Fresh off the relaxation and wonder of their honeymoon, my parents walked into a real estate agency near Lake Cornelia, not too far from the Metropolitan Stadium, where the Vikings played their home games.

"Can I help you?" a white man charged as they walked in the door.

"We're looking for an apartment. Or perhaps a condo," my dad responded.

"Well, we don't have anything in the area right now," he replied politely.

Disappointed, my parents headed back toward the parking lot. A few yards away from their car, another white gentleman called out to them. He happened to also work for the real estate company.

"Hey, you're Gene Washington," he said, recognizing my dad from the newspaper. "I bet you're looking for a place here in Minnesota now that you're joining the team."

"Yes, we are," my dad replied, a bit surprised that the man recognized him.

"But they don't have anything," my mom said as her new-bride fantasy slowly slipped away.

"Oh, we have lots of places. Houses, condos, apartments . . . there are a lot of great things in this area. Let me help you find something," the man replied.

My parents paused and looked at each other as the man continued to solicit their real estate business. My mom described it as the moment she learned about *Minnesota nice*, a kind of racism that smiles in your face and discriminates against you in the same breath. If the man hadn't recognized my dad from the newspaper, they might have been yet another Black couple who couldn't obtain housing in the area because of their skin color. Unlike the South, where there were signs that literally said *White Only*, this was a more covert approach that would take some skill to maneuver.

In time, they would come to learn that the ongoing construction of the interstate highway I-94, funded through the Federal-Aid Highway Act of 1956, had decimated the Rondo neighborhood, a thriving Black business and residential center not far from the Minnesota State Capitol in Saint Paul. The practice of being polite and neighborly while systematically destroying the economic fabric of the Black community (even when an alternative route was proposed by the city engineer) was occurring in Saint Paul long before my parents arrived. Six hundred Black families were displaced, and many of the 300 businesses impacted didn't survive the bulldozers and construction equipment that sliced through their beacon of Black prosperity, leaving a gaping dirt pit that took years to become an interstate highway in 1968.

My parents secured an apartment on the other side of Saint Paul, not far from the stadium. There was barely time to purchase furnishings before my dad was due in Atlanta to play in the Coaches' All-America Game for college all-stars. The game provided some excitement and an opportunity to reconnect with his brothers from MSU, George "Mickey" Webster and Bubba Smith. They clinched a 12–9 victory for the East on July 9, 1967, in Atlanta Stadium, as more incidents of violence raged on in Missouri, Iowa, New Jersey, Connecticut, Pennsylvania, California,

North Carolina, and New York. The unrest even hit close to my parents'
new home on July 19, 1967, in Minneapolis, Minnesota.

That evening, African American youths staged a protest on
Plymouth Avenue in North Minneapolis at the annual Aquatennial
Torchlight Parade, celebrating the beauty of Minneapolis's lakes, riv-
ers, and parks. Oral history and newspaper clippings converge on the
narrative that police abused a 14-year-old Black girl at the parade with
night sticks, which added to ongoing frustration with the police and
the Jewish business owners in the community who mistreated them.

At one time, North Minneapolis had been among the only neighborhoods open to Jewish and Black residents because of restrictive housing covenants. The two groups had lived fairly harmoniously until the
Jewish community saw more economic opportunities and less restric-
tion and discrimination after World War II. This created Jewish flight
to suburban areas and places where they were previously not allowed
to live. Jewish businesses left the North Minneapolis community, and
those that stayed had strained relationships with their Black neighbors.
Stores were burned and vandalized to the tune of $4.2 million over
the course of a few days. The governor, Harold LeVander, deployed
600 Minnesota National Guard members to manage the unrest, which
lasted three days and ended in 36 arrests, including children, and a total
of 24 injuries. Among the arrests were four white citizens involved in
the incidents. The Minnesota National Guard further occupied and
patrolled Black neighborhoods in other parts of Minneapolis and Saint
Paul through July 24, 1967. In the midst of the violence, there were
community members doing their best to keep peace and protect themselves and their families.

The events in Minnesota coincided with police scuffles in Illinois,
North Carolina, Florida, New Jersey, Mississippi, Ohio, New York,
Alabama, Connecticut, Arizona, and Maryland that occurred the same
week. From July 23 to July 28, 41 people died, 2,000 were injured, and
over 4,000 people were arrested during riots in Detroit, Michigan. The

Motor City was occupied by US Army troops and National Guardsmen in response to the endless fires, looting, and disturbances. Among the dead were looters and citizens mistaken for snipers who were shot by the authorities. Black businesses were damaged alongside white ones on the same block, and everyday citizens not involved in the rioting were caught in the crossfire and killed by authorities without consequence. The unrest spread to other parts of Michigan, including Grand Rapids, Pontiac, Flint, Kalamazoo, Mount Clemens, Muskegon, Benton Harbor, Saginaw, and Albion.

With every new incident that unfolded through early August, police forces became increasingly militarized in their tactics to suppress protesters and rioters alike. Chemical Mace, an aerosol tear-gas gun, was used on crowds with increasing frequency. The visuals of police, Army troops, and National Guardsmen in helmets riding tanks through the streets of American cities with their guns drawn as buildings burn in the background resembled, at least symbolically, the images emerging from Vietnam. By the end of the Long, Hot Summer of 1967, only 18 states out of 50 didn't have incidents of racial unrest.

In president Lyndon B. Johnson's 1964 State of the Union Address, he declared a war on poverty. He aimed to not only "relieve the symptoms of poverty, but to cure it and, above all, to prevent it." Unfortunately, the relief, cure, and prevention weren't coming fast enough. The Black Americans expressing discontent via desperate means throughout the nation weren't setting things on fire or throwing rocks and bottles because they were dripping in economic prosperity. They were disillusioned by the symptoms of poverty they experienced every day, and the racial discrimination that interfered with their ability to get jobs, own homes and businesses, and gain education.

President Johnson assembled the federally funded National Advisory Commission on Civil Disorders, also known as the Kerner Commission, to research the source of the unprecedented wave of unrest during the summer of 1967. When the commission had concluded its investigation, the report charged that white racism was a "most funda-mental" cause behind the widespread rioting. The Kerner Commission found that white racism created segregation, discrimination, and deprivation in Black neighborhoods in large cities that the commission referred to as *ghettos*. The report defined a ghetto as "an area within a city characterized by poverty and acute social disorganization, and inhabited by members of a racial or ethnic group under conditions of involuntary segregation."

The commission surmised that white Americans hadn't fully grasped the ways white society was implicated in the ghetto. "White institutions created it, white institutions maintain it, and white society condones it," the report charged. The commission further issued a call to action to the nation to "make good on the promises of American democracy to all citizens—urban and rural, white and black, Spanish-surname, American Indian, and every minority group." While primarily focused on Black-white relations, the report became evidence of the widespread inequality in policing, justice, consumer credit practices, housing, education, voting suppression, and employment discrimina-tion that marginalized groups suffered in the tailwind of civil rights leg-islation that was supposed to uphold their rights as American citizens.

From a modern lens, it's surreal to page through the Kerner report and its findings. The idea that a report commissioned by the United States government acknowledged the impact of white racism, and even cited *white terrorism* as a reason why citizens were turning to violence as a form of protest, is staggering considering the awkward conversations America is still attempting around race in the 21st century. The report warned that the country was moving toward two societies: one Black, one white—separate and unequal. It offered a sense of urgency in the remedies it proposed, warning, "Discrimination and segregation have long permeated much of American life; they now threaten the future of every American."

The specific remedies outlined by the Kerner report are reminiscent of the *Civil Rights '63* publication that MSU president John A. Hannah and the Commission on Civil Rights placed in the hands of the Kennedy administration in 1964. Hours spent interviewing citizens, collecting data, writing memos, and compiling these exhaustive reports were only as useful as the US government's willingness to implement their suggestions. The Kerner report identified the key areas where Black Americans and other groups experienced discrimination: employment, education, and housing. It also suggested strategies for providing economic welfare, improving community relations with law enforcement through proper conduct and patrol practices, and addressing racial bias in the news media.

The *race problem* in the United States has been researched and well documented by the federal government, yet the conditions identified in the Kerner Commission report persist over 50 years later. In 2020, a global movement emerged from the ashes of the uprisings in Minneapolis and Saint Paul. Fires burned across the Twin Cities in response to the murder of George Floyd at the hands of a police officer who kneeled on his neck for 9 minutes and 29 seconds. "Perry," as he was known by his family, or "Big Floyd" by others, was once a Texas high school football and basketball star like my father had been over 50 years ago. I never imagined living through a global pandemic, let alone the experience of watching my now–senior citizen parents live through another public video-recorded murder of one of our Black neighbors, or another summer of nationwide uprisings and military occupation. Fires burned in Brooklyn Center, Minnesota, in 2021, after Daunte Wright, a 20-year-old father, was shot by a police officer who said she mistook her gun for her Taser. Military tanks and armed soldiers were a constant presence during the Brooklyn Center uprising, which coincided with the final days of the trial of the officer who killed George Floyd.

My neighbors and friends complained of frightening encounters with members of white supremacist and hate organizations in their neighborhoods in Saint Paul and Minneapolis. Racist graffiti, vandalism, and taunts became a mainstay in city alleyways and even on murals dedicated to George Floyd and the movement for Black Liberation in our community and throughout the United States. Community patrols have become a form of citizen defense tactics for public safety as we heal from the trauma of racial violence and the continued murders of unarmed Black people by law enforcement, and a surge in hate crimes targeting Asian Americans and Pacific Islander Americans.

In April 2021, president Joe Biden cited white supremacy as a domestic terrorism threat in a televised address to a joint session of Congress. His words were uttered three months after a white mob stormed the United States Capitol on January 6, 2021, beating and killing a police officer and threatening to murder members of Congress as they certified the presidential election. As the images of Confederate battle flags waving on the Capitol grounds and inside its walls poured in online and on the evening news, it was impossible not to wonder what suffering and pain might have been averted if the nation had more thoroughly addressed the threat of white racism in 1968 when the Kerner Commission published their findings.

The end of the Long, Hot Summer of 1967 marked the conclusion of my dad's college football career as he reported for the College All-Star Game in Chicago, Illinois, on August 4. It was the last time he'd play alongside George "Mickey" Webster and Bubba Smith (who won the MVP award) as representatives of their alma mater, Michigan State University. They played with heart but were whooped something terrible by the Super Bowl–winning Green Bay Packers, losing 27–0 at Soldier Field.

CHAPTER

FIFTEEN

O n the banks of the Red Cedar, there's a school that's known to all . . . ," they sang on command in the Vikings cafeteria. Rookie hazing rituals were in full effect, and my dad and his Bobbsey Twin, Clinton Jones, were among the victims required to sing their college fight song in front of the whole team. Lucky for them they knew the MSU fight song, but there were a few rookies who caught hell because they didn't actually know all the words to their school songs. The tone and vibe of the Minnesota Vikings at the beginning of the 1967 season was jovial and spirited. Clinton and my dad leaned on one another and their new teammate from Notre Dame, Alan Page.

The fun-loving Vikings defense veteran and team co-captain, Jim Marshall, took them under his wing, both hazing and helping the new-bies navigate their new digs in Minnesota. My parents' Super 8 films of those early Vikings days, at house parties and other excursions with a new community of players and spouses, show them living their best lives in every frame of the silent reels. Learning more about my dad and all of his Vikings teammates was a fascinating journey, but through-out the hour that I sat down with Jim Marshall, I was floored by his extraordinary life. He's the kind of person who exudes joy through his entire being. The only time I felt his countenance change was when he described the ways they still faced discrimination in the '60s and '70s—even as players in the NFL.

"I'd say seven or eight years of my career, there were certain hotels we couldn't stay in," he explained to me. "I'll never forget the name of this hotel, it was the Peachtree Manor, on Peachtree Street in Atlanta, Georgia. We were getting off the bus to go into the hotel after flying down there, and the manager came out and started screaming, 'No, no, no.' I thought somebody was getting ready to shoot him or rob him or something. I'm looking around to see what he's yelling about, and realized he was saying, 'No Black players!' Meaning me."

In another incident in Houston, Jim recalled standing next to a hotel pool that looked refreshing in the heat as the thought "Man, it would be nice to take a dip over in that water and cool off," fell out of his mouth.

The hotel manager, who happened to be standing next to him, said, "Yeah, you do that, boy, and I'll pour kerosene on it and light it."

Jim Marshall is a *true* African American pioneer in the NFL who preceded my dad and Clinton by seven years. He'd seen it all, including hate mail full of epithets sent to the Vikings organization because he was Black. My dad's teammates John Henderson (University of Michigan), who joined the club in 1965, and Oscar Reed (Colorado State), who arrived shortly after my dad in 1968, remembered feeling like they were going backward with regard to racial progress when they noticed the Vikings wouldn't place Black and white players in the same hotel room when the team was on the road. While my dad and Clinton always thought it was just good fortune and friendship that explained why they were assigned to room with one another for away games, John Henderson and Oscar Reed noticed that even if there were an even number of players, they'd still place the extra white player in a separate room, rather than put him with a Black player.

Even though it was clear that the Vikings organization was awkward at best in the management of racial concerns on the road, the momentum that my dad, Clinton, and Alan Page brought to working with Black veterans like Carl Eller, John Henderson, and Earsell Mackbee contributed to an exciting shift led by head coach Bud Grant, who'd been hired out of Canada in 1967. The Vikings had more losses than wins in 1966 but the team's potential was palpable, even early on in the season. Perfecting their chemistry would take time. My dad was patient, albeit frustrated as he was utilized very little during his rookie year. More than anything, it was hard adjusting to losing. He and Clinton Jones had just come off back-to-back National Championship titles and an undefeated 1966 season. Losing was something he and Clinton weren't comfortable getting used to. It was as if they were college freshmen all over again, eager to make a contribution to the team but unable to do so.

The weather was even colder in Minnesota than it had been for them in East Lansing. Bud Grant forbade gloves, heaters, and other comforts on the sidelines, even on the coldest days when they played in the snow. Training camps took place at a community baseball field that had one toilet for all the players. The team didn't have indoor practice fields, weight facilities, or stunning locker rooms like NFL and college football players have today. It was hard knocks in those days. Even for the spectators.

My mom suffers from Raynaud's disease, a circulation disorder that turns her hands and extremities blue when she's cold. No matter how much she bundled up in the outdoor Met Stadium alongside the other spouses and fans, she'd always leave looking and feeling like a popsicle. Learning how to walk on icy pavement was also a challenge met with a lot of slipping, sliding, and eventually a fall that landed her in the hospital and with stitches in her face.

The Vikings finished the 1967 season with three wins, eight losses, and three ties and finished in fourth place in the NFL Central Division. My dad and Clinton made significant contributions with both playing in all 14 games that season and my Dad averaging 29.5 yards per reception. The team was in the early stages of becoming something special, led by quarterback Joe Kapp, a Mexican American, who joined the team after a trade between the Canadian Football League (CFL) and the NFL.

In the off-season, my dad returned to Michigan State to finish out his student teaching so he could officially graduate and complete his work toward becoming a physical education teacher. My mother was pregnant with my sister Lisa, so she followed my dad for the duration of winter to East Lansing, where she took a few courses toward the completion of her degree. They were very much finding their way as newlyweds between the NFL and the pragmatic responsibilities of completing their education. Things were going great, and the future was feeling extremely bright until things took a turn.

My maternal grandmother, Lula Mae Goudeau, passed away in a Houston hospital on March 22, 1968. The family barely had an opportunity to mourn when Martin Luther King Jr. was killed 13 days later, on April 4, 1968, setting off the Holy Week Uprising in 110 cities throughout the United States just before Palm Sunday.

My sister Lisa was born two weeks later, on April 19. My dad's teammates and MSU classmates made visits to the hospital to check on my mom and welcome my parents' firstborn. My parents successfully convinced my grandfather to let my mom's youngest sister, my aunt Lynette, enroll at Michigan State and help my mom with the new baby when they returned to Minnesota for the football season. Over the summer, they also sent for my mom's nephew Ted, Lisa's godfather, who my dad helped secure a band scholarship to attend MSU. They lived in a small apartment together in East Lansing and balanced my parents' lives in Michigan and Minnesota for a few football seasons, as my mom, her nephew Ted, and Aunt Lynette took classes, and my dad completed a master's degree in college student personnel administration.

President Lyndon B. Johnson's Executive Order 11246, which led to an economic realization that corporations needed to take an "affirmative action" toward leveling the playing field in hiring and employment practices that previously kept diverse employees out of the workforce, created a lane for my dad, and later my mother, to champion diversity in the human resources field. My dad was introduced to 3M because of his new role at Michigan State during the off-season, working as assistant director of student placement services under the direction of Jack Shingleton.

My dad developed a passion for counseling students of color and created channels for them to gain employment through hiring fairs with top companies in Michigan and throughout the country. He even coordinated the university's first minority career fair, possibly one of the first of its kind in the United States. He understood that football wouldn't likely last forever. A career in diversity and inclusion was both urgent for his friends and colleagues looking for employment and also rooted in his understanding that he could make a difference, the way the Smith family and those who'd supported him along the way had made a difference in his life.

One of the most incredible revelations for me is the fact that my dad always had a *day job* while he was playing professional football. During the season he worked part time at 3M Corporation in Minnesota as a human resources recruiter. He'd work all day Monday, then split his time in the office in the mornings Tuesday through Friday, from 7:00 to 11:00 a.m., then he'd report for Vikings football practice. Saturdays the team practiced, then on Sundays they played their games. Even if the Vikings had an out-of-town game on Sunday, he'd be back at 3M first thing Monday morning.

When he returned to Minnesota for the 1968 season, he continued to balance his responsibilities at 3M as the team earned an NFL Central Division title. Unfortunately the Vikings lost to Bubba Smith and his Baltimore Colts 24–14 in the Western Conference Championship Game. The only consolation was that my dad's friend Bubba was able to play in Super Bowl III that year. My dad was still very proud of his

friend from their home state of Texas. Unfortunately the Colts lost to
the New York Jets, and the game itself would be a point of frustration
for Bubba the rest of his life. The Colts were heavily favored to win, and
the game is still viewed as one of the biggest Super Bowl and professional sports upsets ever. The Vikings made a Playoff Bowl appearance,
where the two losers of the Conference Championships played in a
third-place bowl game eight days after the Super Bowl, but they lost
17–13 in a close game against the Dallas Cowboys.

Aside from time spent in East Lansing during the off-season, my
dad and Clinton rarely saw MSU teammates and first-round picks
Bubba Smith or George "Mickey" Webster unless it was on the field
as opponents. Their paths diverged a bit, but they all found their way
in the pros. George Webster wasn't initially thrilled to join the Oilers
because they were a losing team in 1966, but he made a significant
contribution. He was AFL Rookie of the Year in 1967 and made the
All-Star Game in 1967, 1968, and 1969. The Oilers won the AFL Eastern
Division in 1967 and came in second in 1968 and 1969. Bubba played in
both Super Bowl III and Super Bowl V. He made the All-Professional
team in 1971 and was named to two Pro Bowls.

My dad and Clinton were part of the most beloved and successful
Vikings teams in franchise history. By the 1969 season, fans began to call
Alan Page, Carl Eller, Jim Marshall, and Gary Larsen, the formidable
Vikings defensive line, the "Purple People Eaters." Both Alan Page and
Carl Eller have been inducted into the NFL Hall of Fame. In a game
against the Colts on September 28, 1969, quarterback Joe Kapp tied the
all-time NFL record for seven touchdown passes, tying with all-time
greats Y. A. Tittle, Adrian Burk, and Sid Luckman. My dad caught two
of the seven. The Vikings finished the 1969 season with 12 wins and only
2 losses, winning the NFL Central Division title. They faced the LA
Rams in the Los Angeles Coliseum and won the Western Conference
Championship.

The four-year agreement between the AFL and NFL to complete the merger set 1970 as the first season the two leagues would be officially combined. This meant that my dad and his teammates played and won against the Cleveland Browns in the last ever NFL Championship at the end of the 1969 regular season. The game was played at Met Stadium on January 4, 1970, in eight-degree weather with a wind chill below zero. Unless you've experienced it personally, there's no way on earth to describe what eight degrees Fahrenheit feels like in Minnesota. It's the kind of cold that makes you want to cry—but you can't, because your tears will freeze. Bud Grant and his gritty team, with no heaters on the sidelines or gloves on the receivers, beat the Cleveland Browns 27–7.

A few days later, on January 11, 1970, the team traveled to New Orleans for Super Bowl IV for a much warmer 60 degrees with wet conditions on the field. This match also marked a historical moment in the AFL-NFL pre-merger era. The Vikings took on the AFL's Kansas City Chiefs in Tulane Stadium. The Vikings were favored to win by two touchdowns but lost to the Chiefs 23–7. When we met at the Vikings practice facility at Winter Park in 2014 for an interview, my dad's teammate Alan Page—now retired Minnesota supreme court justice Page—shared his reflections about the game when I asked him, "What happened?"

The strength of the Chiefs was evident early in the game. In the first quarter, the defense was stunned when the Chiefs' place kicker, Jan Stenerud, sent a Super Bowl record-breaking 48-yard field goal through the uprights.

"I'm thinking, okay, if they get to the 47-yard line, they can score three points every time. That means if we're going to be in this thing, we've got to keep them at least that far out and probably another 10 or 15 yards. It was not very likely that we were going to keep them from crossing the 50-yard line. *We're in for a fight here*, I thought. And unfortunately we didn't play particularly well on defense and offensively; we didn't score enough points," Justice Page explained with a shrug and a smile.

It was a challenging defeat for the 1969 Vikings. Nevertheless, they'd achieved something as a team in just a few years that the franchise hadn't achieved in its nine-year history. Joe Kapp was named Most Valuable Player for the 1969 season. In his acceptance speech, he refused the honor because as he saw it, all 40 of his teammates were valuable. The team soon adopted the slogan "40 for 60"—40 players playing as one for 60 minutes. Similar to my dad and Clinton's team at MSU, their Vikings teammates, whether Black, white, or in Joe Kapp's case, Mexican American, had become brothers. Under the leadership of Bud Grant they'd turned the franchise around in a matter of a few seasons.

My dad went on to make the All-Professional team in 1969 and 1970, and played in the Pro Bowl in 1970 and 1971. He was the first wide receiver in Vikings history to receive both honors for two consecutive years. The "40 for 60" mindset ushered in another great season for the Vikings in 1970 with 12 wins and only 2 losses again. After the merger, with the AFL and NFL officially becoming the NFL we know today, the Vikings won the first NFC Central title but lost the NFC Divisional Playoffs to the San Francisco 49ers. The 1971 season was almost like déjà vu with 11 wins and 3 losses, and an NFC Central title that ended in an NFC Divisional Playoff loss to the Dallas Cowboys.

My dad was at the top of his game when his five-year contract was up at the end of the 1971 season. He was hopeful that his next contract would be bigger than the first, to account for his success on the team and to support an expanding family with the announcement of my mother's pregnancy with my sister Gina. He was extremely shrewd in how he managed his income from his day job and the income he earned from football. My parents would use my dad's earnings through his employment at 3M and Michigan State for living expenses, but would do their best to only use the football income for my mom's and Aunt

Lynette's tuition or for family emergencies. When his contract was up, he was met with an unexpected decrease in salary.

Jim Finks, the Vikings general manager, offered my dad a new contract at a reduced salary. After a fairly solid 1971 season, my dad, Clinton, and a Black safety named Charlie West started to compare notes about their salaries. Clinton and Charlie called my dad, who was in East Lansing during the off-season, and the three decided to negotiate their contracts as a unit.

"If you sign one of us, you have to sign all of us, is what we told them," Clinton recounted when I asked him about the negotiations. "We were like the three musketeers. We had an agent who Jim Finks wasn't a fan of, but we didn't know it at the time. Gene, Charlie, and I felt we'd be stronger together, so we sat out of training camp until we got what we wanted, a guaranteed contract."

When the Vikings' training camp began in July, my dad, Clinton, and Charlie West remained unsigned. Their teammate John Henderson still hadn't signed a new contract as of July 27, 1972. The challenge that my dad and other players of their era faced was their inability to search for better contracts with other teams because the League operated under the Rozelle rule at the time. The Rozelle rule was named after Pete Rozelle, the NFL commissioner. Under Rozelle in 1972, if a player wanted to go to another team for a better contract or any other reason, the new team would have to compensate the former team with a trade, draft selection, or monetary compensation. If the two teams were unable to agree, Pete Rozelle would decide on the compensation.

Two years prior, in 1970, Joe Kapp was traded by the Vikings to the Boston Patriots after contract negotiations with Jim Finks failed. In order to make the trade, the Patriots had to compensate the Vikings with their first-round draft choice for 1972, and John Charles, a Black defensive back they'd selected first in 1967. Although Joe and his new team executed a memo agreement in 1970, the Patriots demanded he sign a restrictive Standard Player Contract in order to play in 1971.

He refused to sign the contract and was ousted from training camp. The series of events led him to file an antitrust lawsuit against the League, Rozelle, and other relevant parties in 1972. Joe Kapp's lawsuit opened the door to legal actions that would change free agency in the NFL forever.

In 1972, my dad, Clinton Jones, Charlie West, and 12 other players filed a lawsuit led by John Mackey, president of the NFL Players Association, to challenge the Rozelle rule in the United States District Court. Judge Earl Larson ruled in favor of the players in *Mackey v. NFL* on December 30, 1975. The Rozelle rule was found to violate antitrust laws, and the court's judgment acknowledged that the application of the rule damaged players' professional careers. The ruling didn't come in time for my dad or others who retired before or shortly after the court's decision, but their efforts made free agency and multimillion-dollar contracts possible for players today.

Fortunately my dad, Clinton, and Charlie West were able to secure guaranteed contracts with better terms and reported to training late in the summer of 1972. Shortly after the season began, my dad was running a pass pattern and felt a pop in the top portion of his foot. His doctor confirmed that some bone fragments had broken loose. He had two surgeries and missed most of the season while he recovered.

At the beginning of the 1973 season, he played well in an exhibition game and caught some passes. He felt ready and was demonstrably able to make a contribution to his team after a long recovery. In the locker room, Bud Grant called him over and said, "You've been traded to the Denver Broncos. You're no longer with the Vikings."

When my dad told me the story for the first time in 2014, I was dumbfounded.

"Bud said, 'John Ralston, the Denver coach, is a good guy. You'll like playing for John,' and that was it. He thanked me, and then after that, I was on my way to the Denver Broncos," he explained with resignation.

Without warning or notice, his career with the Minnesota Vikings ended before the season unfolded. He shared the startling news with my mom, who was stunned by how abruptly the news was delivered. They'd recently bought their first house in Edina, Minnesota, and they had two children under five years old. Before they could gather themselves to make decisions about how their family would manage a relocation, my dad was on a plane to Denver.

Clinton was furious when he found out that my dad was traded. He was ready to quit the team. My dad attempted to calm him down, and took the news in stride. What could he do? At least the guaranteed contract that they'd secured in 1972 meant that he still had a job. My parents worked it out, and my mom and sisters stayed in Minnesota while my dad commuted to and from Denver during the season. Strangely, my dad's trade to the Broncos foreshadowed what was to come for Clinton.

Like my dad, Clinton was also injured during a practice and fractured his elbow. He nursed himself back to health and became a student of the Silva Method, a self-help practice that he used to visualize his healing. Clinton also believed that the Silva Method gave him clairvoyant abilities, because he had a dream that Bud Grant was going to trade him to the San Diego Chargers.

Like my dad, Bud Grant called Clinton over to him after a practice and said, "Look, we've got ourselves a situation . . ."

Before he could finish, Clinton interrupted him. "You're going to trade me to San Diego?"

Bud looked at him for a while and said, "Wow. You're in the wrong business."

The next day Clinton was on a plane to San Diego. It was impossible not to feel sick to my stomach when I heard how arbitrary my dad's and Clinton's trades were. I couldn't help but wonder if their willingness to fight for fair contracts and participate in a lawsuit against the NFL might have impacted their relationship with Jim Finks and the Vikings organization. At the same time, they were both injured, which makes it even more difficult to diagnose the *why* behind the trades. Hearing their stories for the first time as an adult made me angry about the *how*.

I admittedly hate comparisons between slavery and professional sports in the United States. The NFL and NBA, because of the overwhelming imbalance of Black players and white owners, have been called "plantation systems" by their culture critics. Getting paid to play professional sports and being *enslaved* are vastly different experiences. Out of respect for my ancestors who *were* slaves, I refuse to invoke the comparison. I do, however, acknowledge how dehumanizing the language of being "traded" feels and how under the Rozelle rule, players had little control over what happened to them. The team that signed them was the team that owned the rights to their playing skills until they were injured and couldn't play anymore or they retired.

When I had the opportunity to ask my dad's Vikings teammates how they felt when my dad and Clinton were traded, I could see how deeply the events had touched them.

"Guys come and guys go, and you accept the fact that this was the way the business is run. But these were my friends and it was a sad time. It was a loss. Your dad was one of our biggest threats. We had the fastest guys that played the game," Jim Marshall attempted to explain. "You didn't want to see that happen. Management had changed. The fun that we had and the camaraderie seemed to kind of dissipate. It gave you notice that football is changing and you either change with it or you're going to go."

I was floored by the grace of being able to have such a tender conversation about my dad with Jim Marshall. In my documentary, *Through the Banks of the Red Cedar*, Fred Zamberletti, the team trainer from 1961 to 1998, is on the cusp of tears when he says, "The best years for Gene Washington were before the trade. Maybe with today's medicine, with the fine arthroscope, they could have cleaned that ankle up a bit, and given him more playing time."

My dad made things work with the Broncos, playing out his contract and making a fairly good contribution, but it was frustrating.

"After being traded to Denver, I played one year, and I wasn't 100 percent that year that I played. At the end of that year, I had major surgery where the bones were all fused together, which ended my career. That was the most frustrating part of my career when I first got hurt, my sixth year with the Vikings; I had never been injured in my life. So that was a shock to me. Ninety percent of what I did as a receiver was my speed as a runner—and if you can't run, you can't run your pass patterns. It's hard for you to be successful," my dad explained.

All thanks to the no-cut guaranteed contract that my dad, Clinton, and Charlie West fought for in 1972, during my dad's two years at Denver the Vikings were obligated to guarantee his salary, which they did. He played one year and couldn't play in the second year because his injury got worse. Another full-fusion operation at Mayo Clinic ended his career. My dad retired in 1975 after eight years in the NFL.

Clinton played one year with the San Diego Chargers, then retired in 1973. His marriage to Laverne ended and he stumbled to find his way a bit. He later enrolled in chiropractic school where he met a devout Buddhist named Rosilee. The two have been married more than 40 years and have five daughters, six granddaughters, and a grandson.

Duffy Daugherty's other set of twins, Bubba Smith and George Webster, had nearly a year's more longevity in the League, and were also not immune to the turmoil of injuries and the ways that professional football was becoming a billion-dollar industry. Just like his buddy Gene from La Porte, Texas, Bubba requested a renegotiation of his contract in 1972. During his time with the Colts, Bubba contributed to multiple Super Bowl appearances and helped the team win one. Bubba Smith didn't get what he'd asked for per se, but by the start of the exhibition season he'd settled on new terms with Carroll Rosenbloom, the Colts' owner.

In an exhibition game against the Pittsburgh Steelers, Bubba threw his body at Ron Shanklin to make a tackle but missed, and ran full force into a steel line marker, destroying his right knee. He struggled, as my dad had, to recover from surgeries and rehabilitation. Bubba managed his pain with an alternating combination of black beauties and Quaaludes. On the other side of his injury, he reported to practice for a scrimmage. After practice his coach, John Thomas, called him into his office and delivered the news that he was traded. "You've always talked about California, Smith—you're now an Oakland Raider," Bubba recounted in his memoir.

His stint with the Raiders was brief, and he finished his career with the Houston Oilers in 1976. In 1978 Bubba took on the NFL in a personal injury lawsuit that did not rule in his favor. The effort did, however, result in a rule book change, and line markers are no longer made of steel today. George "Mickey" Webster was traded to the Pittsburgh Steelers when his first contract expired in 1972. He finished his career with the New England Patriots and retired in 1976, after football had taken its toll on his body. Just over 10 years after he retired, George applied for disability benefits with the NFL. His football-related hand, foot, knee, and ankle injuries were life altering but not sufficient to qualify for full disability benefits. One of his legs was amputated above the knee a few years before he died in 2007. His MSU and NFL teammates gathered to mourn the great loss and celebrate his life. One of his Spartan brothers, who shall remain nameless, became the guardian of his cremated remains, and may or may not have made sure that a part of George "Mickey" Webster was returned to the banks of the Red Cedar on the field at Spartan Stadium.

Marcia Livingston, Bubba's college sweetheart, remained a devoted friend even though their romantic relationship didn't survive his first year with the Colts. She had wanted a simple family life in Michigan, and their paths didn't seem to align as a couple. Marcia eventually married and had the family she'd always wanted. When I spend time with her, I can't help but feel like I'm the child she imagined she'd have with Bubba when they were young. The love they shared was full of dreams that were thwarted by the complexities of race and celebrity. Marcia's husband was supportive of her continued friendship with Bubba, which the gentle giant leaned on toward the end of his life.

After he died, Marcia made sure that Bubba's brain tissue became part of the US Department of Veterans Affairs, Boston University, and Concussion Legacy Foundation (VA-BU-CLF Brain Bank) research study of chronic traumatic encephalopathy (CTE), a form of brain trauma related to concussion that's hard to diagnose prior to death. For families who receive a CTE diagnosis after a loved one dies, it offers a subjective bit of hope, or at least an explanation for the mental and emotional challenges their spouses, parents, or children experienced while they were alive.

After the researchers at the Brain Bank studied the CTE in Bubba's brain, they gave it the classification of Stage III CTE with symptoms of cognitive impairment and challenges in judgment and planning. He was the 90th out of 94 NFL players to be diagnosed with CTE after he died in 2011, at age 66. I owe so much to Bubba Smith for his friendship and support of my dad growing up in La Porte, Texas. It's humbling that Bubba left another lasting gift as a participant in the study. Bubba and other former players who've donated tissue will benefit athletes and military veterans through scientific research, and hopefully the prevention of CTE, for generations to come.

In the time since Bubba passed away in 2011, I've been by my dad's side as we've said goodbye to other teammates, coaches, and family members who've died. If I hadn't given my dad a ride to Bubba's home that night years ago, I'm not sure that I would have worked so hard to learn about their history or share it with the world. Time with my dad feels so incredibly precious now. For my own family and the families of many aging football players, CTE is the elephant in the room we hold our breath around. The revelation that players from my father's generation, and some in their 30s, experience cognitive issues in life and are then diagnosed with CTE after death is sobering. It's like living in the post-9/11 era's terror code alerts—hovering at a steady orange "high risk" indefinitely and there's nothing we can do about it.

In 2016, Joe Kapp went public with his Alzheimer's diagnosis. When I interviewed him in 2014, I could tell that his hearing had been diminished. I felt like I was yelling at him with every question, but he was still sharp as a tack. He loves my dad and Clinton with his whole spirit, and he presented every tooth in his mouth like a Cheshire cat when he talked about the two of them and their respective nicknames, "Geno" and "Cadillac Jones." I became friendly with his daughter Gaby, who was attending USC the years that I was filming the documentary, and later his son J. J., who is often by his father's side at reunion events. When Joe Kapp went public with the diagnosis, it was hard not to think about his family and the impact that memory loss can have on a loved one's personality and personal relationships.

The fact that retired players of my father's generation often struggle to get basic health care and other services they need in their old age, as they await the likelihood of a CTE diagnosis once they finally die, is part of the cruel reality football families must endure. Even as benefit programs for retired players expand, the application and claims processes can be extremely difficult to navigate. In May of 2021, retired Washington running back Ken Jenkins and his wife, Amy Lewis, presented a petition with 50,000 signatures to Anita B. Brody, Senior US District Judge in Philadelphia, who presides over the NFL's $1 billion settlement of brain injury claims. Retired players were both exposing and challenging the use of race-norming practices in cognitive assessments of Black players seeking support through the settlement. Race-norming uses a scoring framework that assumes Black men have lower cognitive skills than white men and therefore must perform lower than whites to demonstrate sufficient mental decline to qualify for an award.

When I consider the hardship and racism that players of color face in their youth, and later as they age, I think about the moment that Joe Kapp declined the MVP award in 1969, because he said there wasn't one most valuable Viking, "there are 40 valuable Vikings." I appreciate the contributions they made to the game and the ideals of racial progress in the United States, with full reverence and acknowledgment of the impact to their physical bodies. Many of the older Vikings legends don't attend the reunion events because of health problems. On invited game days, wheelchairs, carts, canes, and walkers make it possible for them to make it to the field in time for a halftime appearance honoring the club's pioneers.

Their physical limitations don't change my sense of affection or interest in their stories. If anything, they make me appreciate every social opportunity we get to spend with one another. I've become my dad's tagalong kid for sporting events and activities. I may have almost caught up with my mom in terms of football-related social-event rushing yards. I think after 50-plus years as a football spouse, she appreciates the time off. I enjoy meeting other football kids and being a fly on the wall to their conversations just as I was when my dad's teammates drew me in at Bubba's home in 2011.

In recent years, the Vikings organization has had more of an "open door" policy with the support of the NFL's initiatives to honor the early pioneers as the Legends Community nationwide. The effort to at least acknowledge the old-timers and the things they've gone through to build the League means that my dad and his teammates are reunited through outreach events during football season and other times of the year.

I love every minute I get to spend with my dad and his teammates. Jim Marshall always greets me with the biggest smile, and I can feel the genuine love and respect that Carl Eller, Alan Page, Oscar Reed, and John Henderson still have for both of my parents. They shared an amazing collective experience that few on the planet can relate to. The odds of them becoming professional football players in the 1960s given the racial climate in America at the time were even slimmer than they are for NFL hopefuls today. They are part of a fraternity that has forever shaped history and pop culture.

CHAPTER
SIXTEEN

I made my way to an empty corner gate in LAX to join my dad on a call with a radio station in Detroit. It was about 6:00 a.m. in Los Angeles, and we were both catching flights—he was on his way to Minneapolis–Saint Paul International Airport when he dialed in. I muted the phone so the overhead announcements at LAX didn't interrupt the call. We were doing press to promote the world premiere of our documentary, *Through the Banks of the Red Cedar*, about my dad's journey from La Porte, Texas, to Michigan State and the NFL.

"I was taken aback that Maya wanted to do all this. She's worked hard and I'm real proud of her. Every day is a gift," he offered the sportscaster and the morning commuters.

I blushed, crouched in the corner with one finger in my ear while someone's cranky toddler had a meltdown at a nearby gate. After six years, at six in the morning, we were 24 hours away from the Gatorade dunk of a lifetime. I'm not even sure if it is possible to quantify the amount of research, fundraising, production, and postproduction that went into my Little Red Hen story about my dad in preparation for our debut at the 2018 *Detroit Free Press* Freep Film Festival.

It was a bittersweet time. The culmination of years of hard work occurred months after former USA Gymnastics and Michigan State

University doctor Larry Nassar was sentenced to 40 to 175 years in prison in January 2018 for the serial sexual abuse of over 150 women and girls who bravely testified in court. I pray that their stories of survival are not forgotten and that their courage will be acknowledged with dignity for generations to come. The horror of their suffering is a stain on Michigan State University's legacy that can never be removed. I continue to grapple with how my dad's opportunity at MSU changed his life for the better in the 1960s, yet the sexual abuse survivors' lives were irrevocably harmed at the institution decades later. The so-called progress of the 1960s did not protect them or keep them safe. With this tension in mind, I hope future generations learn from Michigan State University's leadership during the civil rights movement, as well as the shameful failure in the institution's treatment of student athletes in the 21st century. The ideals of inclusion and equity are only as achievable as our willingness to acknowledge the pain of the past and provide space for both student athletes of my father's generation and the athletes of today to tell their stories.

A scholarship changed my dad's life. The process of making a film gifted us with invaluable quality time and deep connection. The thing I treasured most about the journey was the way that our film provided a platform for players to talk about the indignities they faced during Jim Crow, or the truth of what it was like for early Black pioneers in the NFL. Prior to my taking on the documentary project, my dad had never talked extensively in public about what he and others went through in the 1960s. To my surprise, neither had his teammates.

A few days after we returned from Detroit in 2018, at our sold-out premiere at the Minneapolis–Saint Paul International Film Festival, my dad's Vikings teammate and NFL Hall of Famer Carl Eller shared a story about being turned away from a burger stand as a kid for the audience of 400 during the Q & A session after the film. Standing next to Carl as he described what it was like to be denied service when he had the money to pay for his meal, I realized that perhaps men of their era didn't talk about the past because it was too painful, and also because there wasn't a platform for them to speak about the impact that racism had on their lives.

In the past few years, my dad and I have spent more time together than we have since my early childhood. Instead of car rides to the hardware store or Bridgeman's Ice Cream Shoppe, we're catching flights to share the film and participate in panel discussions with the next generation of athletes and scholars all over the United States. It feels like we've been granted a kind of do-over. I may not have been a track star, but the need to run away from anything and everything related to my dad's connection to sports somehow came back full circle. I relish every new story about his youth and every new factoid about TV time-outs and the new tournament structure for the College Football Playoffs.

The price that my dad and other Black pioneers of his generation and prior paid to make the game what it is today cannot be fully measured. Recent public conversations about the long-term viability of football as we know it, known health risks associated with head injuries, and the role of Black athletes in the game can't be fully unpacked without acknowledging the pioneers. One example is the public reaction to the *Kneel or Stand* debate that erupted in 2016 when San Francisco 49ers quarterback Colin Kaepernick and other NFL players set off all manner of modern media frenzy when they chose not to stand during the national anthem in response to racial discrimination and police brutality. For almost five years leading up to the 2016 football season, a painful experience in Black and brown communities finally had a national platform—not because of Kaepernick, but because cell phone and surveillance cameras bore witness to a litany of names of unarmed Black children and adults shot and killed by police and sometimes by private citizens.

Colin Kaepernick, similar to Rosa Parks, but with a significantly higher income, just got tired of injustice. He didn't feel like standing, and Ms. Parks didn't feel like giving up her seat on a Montgomery bus in 1955. For the first time in my adult life, that I can remember any-way, white people within my personal network and white pundits on television were willfully and publicly talking about race in reaction to the police shootings of unarmed citizens from 2012 to 2016. By fall of 2017, Kaepernick remained unsigned for the season, and a new wave of celebrity Black activists on cable news dominated the airways and online conversations around the national anthem. Some in the Black community called for an all-out NFL boycott until Kaepernick was signed. The quarterback used his platform to help Black communities and others impacted by police violence nationwide and settled with the NFL in 2019, after he'd sued for collusion between teams that refused to sign him. It was fascinating to watch the public debate around the anthem—and race in general—become a form of entertainment on cable news.

Perhaps white people, who still shape the media Americans con-sume, have always been nuanced in their relationship to police violence toward non-white people, but it seemed as if the national conversation unraveled in many directions, between people of a variety of back-grounds, and it gave me an insight that I'd never experienced before. It had been over 50 years since the bodies of James Chaney, Michael Schwerner, and Andrew Goodman were found in an earthen dam in Mississippi, weeks after they were falsely arrested and released by local police who knew the KKK was hunting the three civil rights workers.

The major difference between Mississippi in 1964 and America in 2016 was the 24-hour news cycle—the details playing out on social media in that 21st-century way that American racism serves as a com-modity and a form of entertainment. The tropes of the "racist white killer cop," the "Black super predator thug," and the "entitled million-aire athlete who doesn't respect the flag" were well suited for hours of liberal and conservative cable news programming. My dad and others of his generation were part of both the civil rights struggles of the 1960s and the push for players' rights in the 1970s, which made it possible for

Kaepernick and his contemporaries to gain million-dollar salaries and the right to free agency.

The most frustrating thing about the media fodder around the national anthem was that all the talking heads weren't actually *doing* anything to address bias in policing or the real concerns of the men who built the League. At the height of the national anthem firestorm, I was struggling to raise funds for my film about the racial integration of college football. I wondered if the angry white pundits and the Black men picketing in front of the NFL headquarters in New York even knew about the Rozelle rule, *Mackey v. NFL*, or that my dad and others had risked everything to make free agency possible for Kaepernick and other players today. It was palpable how the nature of my familial relationship to the NFL impacted my perception of the organization. As much as the media made it a *Black* and *white* issue, it was an extremely nuanced moment for me.

The women and people of color at the highest levels of the League and the Vikings organization were critical to my ability to complete and release *Through the Banks of the Red Cedar*. I faced an uphill battle as a Black woman making a football movie about a chapter in history that even Michigan State University had done little to celebrate. I had to maneuver through the financial expense of licensing agreements for the right to use archival footage of my father and his teammates in my film, on top of years of production and postproduction costs as an independent filmmaker. When I sat in the lobby of the NFL headquarters in New York, waiting to screen a rough cut of the film in 2017, I realized that I'd never in my life been in any professional business environment with so many Black men, women, and people of color walking around the office. The external perception of the League being all-white was what I was expecting, but it wasn't what I actually encountered. There was a dissonance when it came to the public perception of the NFL as an employer that even I'd been susceptible to.

I wouldn't likely have made a film or written this book if my dad hadn't played in the League. A lot of the opportunities I've had in life because of my dad's employment as a professional football player might not have existed, including the opportunity to pursue a career in the arts. My dad's professional football career provided an economic foundation for our family, even if he averaged about $25,000 to $35,000 per year, in contrast to the million-dollar contracts players receive today. The price he paid with his body and the impact those sacrifices had on me and future generations are part of an irreconcilable tension.

Now when I attend games with my dad and put my hand over my heart during the anthem, I think about the private indignities he and his most celebrated teammates endured for the game and the legacy they've left for future generations. For hundreds of years, the United States has attempted to stitch herself together like every symbolic star added to the flag. My African and indigenous ancestors bore the brunt of this colonial injury. Any grace afforded me has been the result of the moral or political awakening of those who oppressed them, and the courage, faith, and resilience of a bloodline that willed me into existence.

~

In 2019, as I drove my dad and Clinton Jones to a restaurant in Eagan, Minnesota, where Debra Jones and Tracy McDonald, who coordinate player outreach and alumni events for the Minnesota Vikings, had arranged a lunch with Bud Grant, it was hard not to catch a few butterflies when I navigated to the wrong venue. Debra, one of our biggest champions within the Vikings organization, coordinated a double feature of *Through the Banks of the Red Cedar* for Black History Month. We had spent the morning with a group of teens, who'd been bused to the massive new training facility. We knew we'd have a nice lunch before heading back for an afternoon screening for the Vikings staff, players, and alumni, but we didn't realize that Debra had invited Bud Grant to lunch with us.

I was doubtful that he'd actually show up. Even after producing a film over the course of six years, I'd still never *met* him. I *saw* him at a 2016 alumni event celebrating the newly built cathedral called the U.S. Bank Stadium, but I didn't know how I *felt* about him. He gave my dad his first job, then traded him after he was injured. It didn't help that one of the Black players I ran into at the 2016 event dropped a little unsolicited nugget in my ear: "Bud used to trade the Black guys. The white ones would get injured—and he'd let them stay."

I observed Bud interacting with my dad and Clinton very little at the 2016 reunion. I kept my distance, but I took a photo on my cell phone for nostalgia. Later when all the Ring of Honor members posed for a photograph on the field, Bud grew impatient and shuffled back to the cart that was used to transport him to the sideline. I recorded the moment with my phone. He continued to pad away from the group as they threw up their arms. "Ahh, come on, Bud . . ." He was still a mythological character who also seemed a bit grumpy in my mind.

Years later when my dad, Clinton, and I finally arrived at the restaurant for lunch, we were greeted by Bud and his girlfriend, seated at the table with Tracy and Debra. It's weird to consider how my heart was pounding or how protective I somehow felt toward my dad. There wasn't anything that Bud could necessarily do to him, but I was timid and introduced myself to his companion, then nodded at him in acknowledgment across the table.

Over salmon and grilled veggies, I watched as Bud gleefully talked about hunting.

"Yeah, I was up in the tree stand for hours. A guy was supposed to pick me up, but he didn't show up until after it got dark."

"What did you do all that time?" I asked.

"Well, I sat there. Not much else I could do," he said with a shrug.

I found him amusing, but my smile faded when my gaze shifted to my dad's arthritic hands pushing the fork around his plate. They looked like the feet of Big Bird from *Sesame Street*, crooked and stiff after years of football, and playing with no gloves out in the cold. The conversation unfurled like a banner in a halftime show when the dessert arrived. Bud shared his thoughts about concussions and his belief that some people might be predisposed to CTE. Somehow, I got up the courage to ask him how he'd heard about my dad and Clinton.

"I knew Duffy Daugherty because he had those clinics. I went to one of them once, up in Bemidji or something. It was close to Canada," he said.

"What were the clinics like?" I asked, eager to hear firsthand what the famous Coach of the Year Clinics were all about.

"Well, they did a whole lot of drinking—and I wasn't into that. I was there to talk about football, and learn something. They were using it like it was their time to get away and slack off."

We all chuckled, knowing what he said was likely true. The restaurant manager, clearly a Vikings fan, came over to the table at least three times during our meal. On the third visit, he asked us to take a photo in the back dining room full of Vikings memorabilia, so he could put it next to the other frames on the wall.

"If you're such a big fan, then you should give us a discount," Bud said, giving the manager a hard time.

He was intense, but likable. I was so grateful that Tracy and Debra had arranged the lunch. My dad and Clinton seemed to be at ease throughout the little reunion as well.

Bud continued to talk about following my dad's and Clinton's careers at Michigan State and the logistics of holding the 1967 draft in Jim Finks's hospital room. He told the story of how the management gave him a hard time when he selected Alan Page as the third pick for the team.

"It came up in the room—I won't say who said it, but it came up that no one's ever done that. No one's ever had three Black guys in the top three picks," he said.

It was the first time I'd heard the story. I'd only known about the phone call my dad received when he was drafted, which he shared as they ate ice cream sundaes and chocolate cake.

"Yeah, Bud. I got a call from a guy congratulating me. And I didn't know who he was," my dad said with a laugh.

"Well, who was he?" Bud asked in that way that older people become impatient with stories that take too long.

"Sid Hartman. From the *Star Tribune*. I didn't hear from the Vikings until a few days after that," my dad said, as they all shared a laugh.

Knowing what they'd been through, their time at Michigan State, and later the uncomfortable and abrupt way things ended was a bit overwhelming as I sipped the rest of my iced tea and thanked the waitress when she cleared my plate.

Then, out of what felt like nowhere, Bud offered, "The most difficult thing about being a coach is making decisions that affect people's lives. Other people didn't see it like I did, but I always made sure I did it myself. That I was the one who delivered the news."

Without specifying that he was referring to my dad and Clinton being traded, the three of us knew what he meant. It was a lot to take in. Who gets the opportunity to revisit their past and come to a different understanding about it? I could tell when the three of them posed for the restaurant manager's photo that Bud had a lot of love for both my dad and Clinton. For the hour or so we spent with him at lunch and later when he joined us for the Q & A after our film screening, he wasn't the steel-eyed, cold *jerk* who traded my dad to the Denver Broncos. He was a deeply complex older man who genuinely loved football. The film gave him an insight into my father's and Clinton's journeys that he and others who work for the organization today wouldn't have known if we hadn't brought their history to light through the documentary.

On the way home my dad said, "I talked to Bud more today than I did in the five or so years I played for him—or the years since."

I shook my head in awe as I made my way onto the freeway. Nowadays I'm almost always the driver and my dad is *my* passenger. We had a laugh about how we'd driven to the Vikings facility that morning in the midst of a snowstorm, and how on the way home the roads were clear, as if it had never snowed at all. We listened to the Temptations Radio on my streaming music service as we made our way through the rush hour commute.

It was hard not to consider the grace that the last few years taught us—like the Black National Anthem, *full of the hope that the present has brought us.* My dad says the most important thing a player can do in a game is focus on his assignment. The advice seems to hold true in life as well. The very thing I was running from during my childhood was the one thing that fused us back together.

We pulled up to the senior apartments my parents moved into after they downsized and sold my childhood home. I put the car in park in the building's driveway.

"Thanks for coming today, Dad," I said as he unbuckled his seat belt.

"Well, thanks for the ride, Coach. Today was fun."

I leaned over and gave him a hug before he exited and started walking to the automatic doors. He turned back toward the car and waved as I pulled onto the main road.

ACKNOWLEDGMENTS

I want to express my gratitude for:

My parents, Gene and Claudith Washington, for their love and sacrifices. My sisters, Lisa and Gina; nieces, Kayla, Ashley, and Rayna; and brothers-in-law, Will and Francis, for their love, patience, and support for the film and now this book. My paternal and maternal grandparents, aunts, uncles, and cousins on earth (and those in heaven) for love, guidance, protection, and the gift of belonging to one another thousands of years after our ancestors dreamed us into existence.

The 1965 and 1966 Michigan State Spartans football and track and field teams, coaches, faculty, staff, classmates, families, and fans. The Minnesota Vikings of the 1960s and 1970s, coaches, staff, families, and fans. All the sports writers, journalists, scholars, and historians who've sought to preserve and uplift untold stories in American sports history.

Angel ancestors Bubba Smith and Benny L. Williams, whose love, courage, and friendship inspire me every day.

The team at Little A: Carmen Johnson, Emma Reh, Emily Freidenrich, Rosanna Brockley, and Merideth Mulroney.

My gratitude to acquiring editor Hafizah Geter, and developmental editor Mosi Secret.

Running Water Entertainment, LLC: Julia Ramadan, Taylor Briese, and Nicole LaPoint.

With humility, I honor and acknowledge the brave survivor athletes who've fought for accountability and justice in the state of Michigan and around the United States. Thank you for your courage and resilience. May your truth always ring louder than anything or anyone that dares to silence your voices.

The National Football Foundation, the College Football Hall of Fame, the Big Ten Conference, the Minnesota Vikings, and the National Football League. Arizona State University Global Sport Institute; California State University, Fullerton; the College of Saint Scholastica; Iowa State University; Michigan State University; Minnesota State University, Mankato; Roanoke College; the University of Minnesota, Duluth; and the University of Southern California Annenberg Institute of Sports, Media & Society.

For support of my lyric hybrid essay "Project Artifacts: Through the Banks of the Red Cedar," which first appeared in a special sports issue of *Prairie Schooner* (Winter 2015) and later appeared in *Bodies Built for Game: The* Prairie Schooner *Anthology of Contemporary Sports Writing* (2019), from the University of Nebraska Press, thank you to Kwame Dawes, Natalie Diaz, Hannah Ensor, and *Prairie Schooner* for those beautiful collections.

For early reads and kindness: Charif Shanahan, Meghan Maloney-Vinz, Michelle Whittaker, and Terry Horstman. For creative community and friendship: Aaron Levy Samuels, Aimee K. Bryant, Ana Kelly, Andrea

Jenkins, Anisha Acharya, Ashaki M. Jackson, Avery R. Young, Bao Phi, Beth Mayer, Bettina Judd, Brian Francis, Byron Marc Newsome, Cedric Tillman, Clarence Livingston, Craig Laurence Rice, Curtis Caesar John, David Lawrence Grant, Deborah Keenan, DéLana R. A. Dameron, Devi S. Laskar, Dwayne Brown, Ed and Mary Bock, Edgar P. Davis, Efren and Nicholas Cornejo-Cacarnakis, Elisabeth Houston, Erika Gilchrist, F. Douglas Brown, F. Michael Young, Gary and Melissa Poux, George Keller, Hannah Foslien, Fredd Parr, Hawona Sullivan Janzen, Herschel and Hansel Pombo McPherson, Jacie Knight, Jacqueline Taylor, Jamie Burton-Oare, JoAnna Rhambo, Jowan Carbin, Jen March, Jonterri Gadson, JP Howard, Julie Heaton, Khadijah Queen, Karin Rosen Hoblit, Kelli Stevens Kane, Khary Jackson, Kimberly Elise, Kongit Farrell, Kymani Kahlil, Kyla Marshell, L. Lamar Wilson, Lester and Toni Purry, Lisa Gopman, L'Oréal Snell, Maria Isa, Mary Moore Easter, Maya Gaddie, Melanie Bullock, Natalie Graham, Natalie King, Nicole Cardona, Niki Williams, Nikki Bailey, Patricia Straub, Phillip B. Williams, Qiana Towns, Rickey Laurentiis, Rio Cortez, Robin Coste Lewis, Rodney and Freda Hobbs, Ronald Schultz, Ron and Becca Johnson, Sami Schalk, Safia Jama, Sarah Bellamy, Selina Lewis, Shameka Allen, Shelby Stokes, Sherilyn Howes, Sherina Rodriguez Sharpe, Sherrie Fernandez-Williams, Shon Fuller, Sofia Mohammad Khan, Su Love, T. Ashanti Mozelle, T. Mychael Rambo, T'ai Freedom Ford, Tiffany Alston, Tina Nagata Barr, Tisa Bryant, Tobias Knight, the Jones family, Van Hayden, and Whitney Lawless. The Los Angeles, New York, and Twin Cities literary, theatre, and film communities, and every cohort, collaborator, mentor, friend, and kindred creative soul who has crossed my path.

Appreciation to Alan Haller; Alan Page; Andie L. Phillips; Anthony and Rhonda Smith; Barton Warren; Bennie Fowler; Bill Friedman; Bill and Gigi Wehrwein; Bill Beekman; Bilquis Dairkee; Bob and Sonali Sur; Brett Taber; Bryn Lambert; Bud Grant; the Bullough family; Carl Eller; Cheryl Gilliam; Chuck Foreman; Clinton Jones; Craig Murray; the Dantonio family; Dan Daugherty; Darien Harris; Darqueze Dennard; Das Campbell; Dave Elliott; Dave Osborn; David Techlin; Debra Jones; Delilah Reynolds; DLP family; Don and Carol Knutson; Don Moorer; Don Weatherspoon; Dree Daugherty Hudson; Eddie Stephens; Edna Boone; Elizabeth O'Neill-Harris; Erin Broome; Ernie Pasteur; Fred and Elizabeth Blalock; Fred Zamberletti; Freda Payne; Gloria Pillow; Greg Coleman; Gregory Reed; Helen Jones; Ian and Frené Chestnut; Isaiah Lewis; Jacklyn E. West; Jeanelle Austin; Jeanette Rupert; James Montague; Jeremy Morris; Jerry Jonckheere; Jill Lombardi; Jim Eaton; Jimmy Raye; Jim Summers; Jim Marshall; Jim Proebstle; Jerry West; Joe Kapp; John Charles; John Henderson; John Mullen; Joseph Brown; Julee Burgess; Karen Olsen Edwards; Karen Sadler; Karin Nelsen; Kimberly Haynes; the Kelly family; Kevin Warren; Kia Bible; the Lance family; Leslie Cooper Johnson; Lillian Edwards; Lonnie Snell; Lynn Makay; Mandy Lee Sperstad; Marcia Howard; Marcia Livingston; Marcus Huggans; Mary Ann McDonald; Mary Gay and the Black community of La Porte, Texas; MaryLou Moore; Matthew Wilcox; Micajah Reynolds; Michelle Lawless; Mick Tingelhoff; Monterae Carter; Myrna Carr; Naomi Hill; Nick Maddox; Oscar Reed; Pat Gallinagh; Pat Mullen; Patrick and Janet Scheetz; Paulette Martis; Renee Dorn; Rickey Young; Robert West; Rochelle Dorn-Hayes; Sandra Morgan; Scherrie Payne; Seth Kesler; Shani Malcolm; Sharon Kaster; Shelmina Babai Abji; Sherm and Toni Lewis; Susan Simons; Sterling Armstrong; Steve Culp; Steve Juday; Syreeta Greene; Ted Bertrand; Tony Sanneh; Tracy McDonald; and the 2013 Michigan State Spartans football team, coaches, staff, and parents. Warren Singleton and the Black community of Baytown, Texas; the families of McNair Station, Texas; the community at 38th and Chicago in Minneapolis, Minnesota; the Walles family; the Watts family; William Ware; Vince Carillot; Vincent and Georgette Harris; YPC;

Xavier and Nicole Porter; and all friends, neighbors, and loved ones of the Washington family.

Through the Banks of the Red Cedar documentary First-In Club, MSU alumni on planet Earth, and you, (insert your name) _____, and every person who has supported these teams, this history, and the work we've done together on film, in literature, and in the classroom. Your support has made it possible for this story to reach people around the world. Whether you've donated to the work, organized an event, attended a screening, sent a kind email, told a friend, or purchased this book, you've made a difference. Thank you for taking this journey with me and my family.

A NOTE ON SOURCES AND FURTHER READING

Shortly after attending the memorial celebration for Bubba Smith in August of 2011, I began what has become a lifelong research quest in search of my father's history. I started with the various books on my father's bookshelf in his man cave, den, and "trophy" room in the lower level of my childhood home. Duffy Daugherty's memoir, *Duffy: An Autobiography*, by Duffy Daugherty with Dave Diles and an introduction by Howard Cosell, and Lynn Henning's *Spartan Seasons: The Triumphs and Turmoil of Michigan State Sports* were key to understanding how and where the 1960s landed in Spartan history. Bubba Smith's 1983 memoir *Kill, Bubba, Kill!* provided insight into the man I'd only known as Moses Hightower from the *Police Academy* movies.

Interviews with my father's teammates, coaches, friends, extended family, and historians helped broaden my view of what happened on the banks of the Red Cedar long before I was born. From 2012 to 2016, I interviewed nearly everyone willing to sit down and chat with me about their memories of MSU and my dad during his time with the Minnesota Vikings. The interviews occurred formally or informally by phone, in person, and on camera. I interviewed both of my parents, my siblings, nieces, aunts, and uncles. Many of those interviews appear in the documentary film *Through the Banks of the Red Cedar* and support the historical narrative of this book. I interviewed my father's MSU teammates Clinton Jones, Dave Techlin, Dick Berlinski, Don Weatherspoon, Ernie Pasteur, Jerry West, Jim Summers, Jimmy Raye, Pat Gallinagh, Sterling Armstrong, and William "Pops" Ware, a few of their spouses, and the children of Jim Summers and Clinton Jones. My father's MSU coaches, Henry "Hank" Bullough and Vince Carillot, and their spouses, Lou Ann Bullough and Lucy Carillot, were extremely gracious in offering time and answering my many questions. The entire Bullough family has been of great support in documenting the MSU teams of the 1960s. The children of Duffy Daugherty, "Danny" and Dree, gave powerful and touching on-camera interviews. Friends of Bubba Smith and George "Mickey" Webster, Edna Boone, John Charles, Joseph Brown, and Marcia Livingston were extremely helpful in filling in parts of the gentle giants' personal stories in Texas, at Michigan State, and beyond. Sisters and legendary recording artists Freda Payne and Scherrie Payne joined me for interviews about their memories of Michigan and MSU in the 1960s. Many classmates, track and field teammates, fans, and former staff of MSU shared their favorite memories from the 1960s over the past 10 years. I cherish every new story uncovered.

My father's teammates and colleagues from the Minnesota Vikings organization, Alan Page, Carl Eller, Dave Osborn, Greg Coleman, Jim Marshall, Joe Kapp, John Henderson, Mick Tingelhoff, Oscar Reed, and Fred Zamberletti, graced me with on-camera interviews. The Minnesota Vikings supported these connections and have demonstrated a sincere desire to uphold the legacy and celebrate the contributions of men of my father's generation. I'm grateful for NFL Films compilations like *The History of the Minnesota Vikings*. Joe Kapp's Memoir *A Life of Leadership: Joe Kapp, "The Toughest Chicano"* with his son J. J. Kapp, Robert G. Phelps, and Ned Averbuck, and the collaborative works of Alan Page and his daughter Kamie Page—*Alan and His Perfectly Pointy Impossibly Perpendicular Pinky*, *Bee Love*, and *The Invisible You*, which support scholarships and education—are near and dear to my heart as examples of family efforts to celebrate and preserve history and culture. The various events my father and I attended from 2011 to the present have allowed for continued conversation and opportunities to learn more about my father's teammates and their families.

Former Michigan State head coach Mark Dantonio, wife Rebecca, and children Kristen and Lauren were gracious in sharing their experiences as a football family. Their friendship and witness to the experience of being a football family of "all girls" remains a blessing to my personal journey of discovery. Members of the 2013 Michigan State Spartans football team, including Bennie Fowler, Isaiah Lewis, Max Bullough, Micajah Reynolds, and their parents provided insight into how the game has changed and the ways that my father's generation paved the way for players today. Getting to know them gave me a glimpse into what my father's life as a student athlete might have been like from 1963 to 1967.

My parents' siblings, former classmates, and the community in La Porte and Baytown, Texas, have been important sources over the years. Betty Lewis Moore, David Janda, Mary Gay, M. L. Phillips, and Warren Singleton are among community members in the region who've preserved Black history in my parents' hometowns. My cousin, Dr. Harlan Mark Guidry, has preserved a great deal of Creole history and culture in both Texas and Louisiana. His advocacy through St. Augustine Historical Society and National Grand Family Heritage Foundation supports continued scholarship and preservation of Creole heritage.

Historians like Johnny Smith, PhD, and Jack Ebling have long studied and written about the era. Both honored me with formal on-camera interviews. I was first introduced to Johnny Smith through my documentary film's consulting producer Selina Lewis, who uncovered his 2006 Western Michigan University master's thesis, "Black Power in Green and White: Integration and Black Protest in Michigan State University Football, 1947-1972." His research and findings later appeared in *Breaking the Plane: Integration and Black Protest in Michigan State University Football During the 1960s*, published in *Michigan Historical Review* by Central Michigan University in 2007. I reached out to Dr. Johnny Smith for an interview for the film and he agreed. His insights and scholarship are a great starting point for anyone who wishes to investigate this time period and its modern implications over 50 years later. I am grateful for his painstaking work to document the hometowns of my father's African American teammates, and other early pioneers at Michigan State University. He currently serves as a "Bud" Shaw Professor of Sports History at Georgia Tech and is the author of several books about sports and history.

Jack Ebling, a Michigan sports broadcaster and writer, reached out to me a few years into my documentary journey. His perspective as a youth who grew up watching my dad and his teammates at the peak of their success at Michigan State as well as his enthusiasm for the university's sports history were fertile ground for my continued inquiry into this subject. His book, *Heart of a Spartan: The Story of a Michigan State Football Renaissance*, was released in 2012. Jack is the author of several books and his radio show, *The Drive with Jack Ebling*, and TV show, *Press Pass with Jack Ebling*, are popular in Mid Michigan among local and regional sports fans.

Another historian, Tom Shanahan, has made a significant contribution to the preservation of this era. His book, *Raye of Light: Jimmy Raye, Duffy Daugherty, the Integration of College Football, and the 1965-66 Michigan State Spartans*, a collaboration with my dad's teammate and quarterback Jimmy Raye, was released in 2014.

In my research about the legacy of John A. Hannah, the former MSU president's memoir, *A Memoir*, first published in 1980 by Michigan State University Press, was critical to uncovering the early years of the school and the foundation that was built before my father arrived in 1963. *The Student and His Professor*, a gem of a book published by the author David J. Young in 2015, as well as his 2011 book *Arrogance and Scheming in the Big Ten: Michigan State's Quest for Membership and Michigan's Powerful Opposition* are thorough and well cited accounts of MSU's efforts to gain entrance into the Big Ten Conference. Although I discovered both books after my film *Through the Banks of the Red Cedar* was released, Young's passionate insights and research provide a solid and fascinating understanding of John A. Hannah and the early years of Big Ten athletics. Young's contribution to this foundational history is significant and worthy of investigating to fully contextualize the history and evolution of the Big Ten Conference.

The physical and digital archives of the Michigan State University Archives and Historical Collections were extremely helpful in the process of making the film and writing this book. I spent hours in the physical papers and ephemera from MSU's founding to the 1970s, focusing on John A. Hannah, Duffy Daugherty, the 1966 Rose Bowl, football, track and field, and student life from the 1960s. The digital collection of games and photographs has been a significant resource over the years. Additionally, time spent watching key football games and track reels from the 1960s deepened my access to my father's history.

Iowa State University journalism professor Brenda Witherspoon was an important spark in my inquiry into the Black football pioneers in the Midwest who preceded my father's teams. When she reached out to engage my father and me in conversation with her academic community in support of the legacy of Jack Trice at the institution, I was humbled by his story, and inspired to include Black players who have yet to receive full honor in American football history in this book. The work of Dr. Daniel Durbin at USC Annenberg Institute of Sports, Media & Society, Kenneth L. Shropshire at Arizona State University Global Sport Institute, and others is important to the preservation of historical narratives in America and around the world. I'm grateful that all three institutions have engaged their academic communities in dialogue about the integration of college football and about my work.

The National Football Foundation and College Football Hall of Fame are important resources in the documentation and preservation of Black history in the game. Visits to the College Football Hall of Fame and the various digital and print publications of the National Football Foundation are important to continued scholarship and public education.

The Library of Congress, the United States Department of Justice, the John F. Kennedy Presidential Library and Museum, Vanderbilt Television News Archive, Wazee Digital, XOS Digital, NFL Films, Shutterstock, Getty, and the Minnesota Historical Society archives were valuable resources in my research and discovery.

In addition to combing through newspaper and magazine articles from the 1940s to the present in publications like the *Lansing State Journal*, *Star Tribune*, *New York Times*, *Sports Illustrated*, *Time* magazine, and others, and bins of dogeared vintage *Life* magazines at a thrift store in South Pasadena, California, I surrounded myself with the voices of Angela Y. Davis in *Women, Race, & Class*, Natasha Trethewey in *Memorial Drive: A Daughter's Memoir*, James Meredith with William Doyle in *A Mission from God: A Memoir and Challenge for America*, and Sharon Robinson in *Child of the Dream: A Memoir of 1963*, and others, reading for pleasure and to gain intergenerational perspective.

ABOUT THE AUTHOR

Photo © 2021 Ed Bock

Maya Washington is an award-winning narrative and documentary filmmaker (writer/director/producer), actor, writer, poet, creative director, photographer, and arts educator. She is dedicated to social impact stories that illuminate aspects of the human experience that are untold or rarely seen or that might benefit from new approaches to issues of diversity and inclusion. For more information visit www.throughthebanksoftheredcedar.com.